Winning Chess Tactics

Yasser Seirawan
International Grandmaster,
with Jeremy Silman

PUBLISHED BY
Microsoft Press
A Division of Microsoft Corporation
One Microsoft Way
Redmond, Washington 98052-6399

Library of Congress Cataloging-in-Publication Data pending.

Printed and bound in the United States of America.

1 2 3 4 5 6 7 8 9   MLML   0 9 8 7 6 5

Distributed to the book trade in Canada by Macmillan of Canada, a division of Canada
Publishing Corporation.

A CIP catalogue record for this book is available from the British Library.

Microsoft Press books are available through booksellers and distributors worldwide. For further
information about international editions, contact your local Microsoft Corporation office. Or
contact Microsoft Press International directly at fax (206) 936-7329.

The photographs in Part 2 are from *A Picture History of Chess,* by Fred Wilson, courtesy of
Dover Publications, Inc.

Acquisitions Editor: Dean Holmes
Project Editor: Tara Powers-Hausmann
Editing and Production: Online Press, Inc.

In memory of Mikhail Tal.

Contents

Acknowledgments   vii

Introduction   ix

PART 1   Tactics and Combinations

CHAPTER ONE	Definitions	3
CHAPTER TWO	The Double Attack	9
CHAPTER THREE	The Pin	35
CHAPTER FOUR	The Skewer	47
CHAPTER FIVE	King Tactics and Combinations	51
CHAPTER SIX	Deflection	73
CHAPTER SEVEN	Battery on an Open File or Diagonal	79
CHAPTER EIGHT	The Power of Pawns	89
CHAPTER NINE	The Decoy	99
CHAPTER TEN	Clearance Sacrifice	105
CHAPTER ELEVEN	X-Rays and Windmills	111
CHAPTER TWELVE	Zwischenzug	117
CHAPTER THIRTEEN	Other Kinds of Draws	119

PART 2   Great Tacticians and Their Games

CHAPTER FOURTEEN	Adolf Anderssen (1818–1879)	135
CHAPTER FIFTEEN	Paul Morphy (1837–1884)	145
CHAPTER SIXTEEN	Rudolf Spielmann (1883–1942)	151
CHAPTER SEVENTEEN	Frank Marshall (1877–1944)	157
CHAPTER EIGHTEEN	Alexander Alekhine (1892–1946)	163
CHAPTER NINETEEN	Mikhail Tal (1936–1992)	175
CHAPTER TWENTY	Garry Kasparov (1963–)	185

PART 3   More Tests and Solutions

CHAPTER TWENTY-ONE	Basic Tactics	199
CHAPTER TWENTY-TWO	Advanced Combinations	201
CHAPTER TWENTY-THREE	Professional Combinations	203
CHAPTER TWENTY-FOUR	Solutions to Tests from Part 1	205
CHAPTER TWENTY-FIVE	Solutions to Tests from Part 3	223
Glossary		235
Index		249

Acknowledgments

Once again, I am much indebted to the many people who labored with me on this effort. Thanks to Michael Franett for supplemental text and finishing touches, and to Eric Woro for eagle-eye proofreading and editorial suggestions. And, of course, thanks to all the folks at Microsoft and Online Press who saw this book through to completion, particularly Tara Powers-Hausmann, Joyce Cox, Larry Powelson, Dean Holmes, and Eric Stroo. You were all terrific.

Introduction

I n my first book, *Play Winning Chess*, I discussed the history of chess and introduced the basic rules and strategies of the game. Teaching chess to beginners is an exercise in creativity. The teacher can go about the task in myriad ways. Some teachers might explain the rules and how the pieces move and then use the world's great chess games—especially their own—as examples. Others might focus on how to play certain openings or how to checkmate. Though all of these methods may eventually lead to an understanding of the basics, some methods produce quicker results than others. In *Play Winning Chess*, I chose the most direct path. I broke down the game of chess into its four elements—force, time, space, and pawn structure—and showed how these elements can be combined to produce a number of principles of play—principles I deduced from studying thousands of master games. Understanding the four elements helps you understand the moves of the masters and inspires you to formulate plans of action in your own games.

After you've grasped the basics, it's time to go to the next level of chess and explore the world of tactics. Only then can you fully appreciate the beautiful combinations that a mastery of tactics allows you to create. Whereas teaching beginner-level chess takes creativity, teaching tactics is a matter of conveying classical knowledge. The teacher can package this knowledge and spin it out in a variety of ways, but the knowledge is basically the same.

Winning Chess Tactics won't teach you anything about tactics and combinations that the chess world doesn't already know. However, I've found that accessing this knowledge about these concepts can be anything but easy. Few of the books that teach combinative play explain tactics and combinations in an instructive manner. The rare exceptions tend to be for advanced players, making a study of this subject rather difficult for those with less experience. In this book, I divide tactics into themes, which I thoroughly explain and illustrate. Each chapter starts out with a discussion of the basic forms of the theme and progresses to increasingly more complex examples. This teaching technique allows for easy learning at the lower levels but also continues instruction right up to the master class. My goal is to enlighten beginner and tournament player alike!

Teaching for such a range of player strength has its drawbacks. For example, I don't stop to explain every chess term that I need to use, and as a result beginners will have it a little tougher here than in the first book. I expect you to have some basic chess knowledge. In particular, you should know the following:

- How the pieces move
- The rules of the game
- How to read and write algebraic chess notation
- How to count the force (the value of the pieces)
- Basic chess terminology
- The four elements of chess and their associated principles, as expounded in *Play Winning Chess*

For lower-level players who might stumble over the chess terms in this book, I've provided a glossary. My advice is to avoid skipping over terms that you are unfamiliar with. Look them up. Take the time to understand each term, and you'll be able to take this book in stride.

A word about terminology of a different sort: Things haven't changed much in the chess world since I wrote *Play Winning Chess* a year ago. Chess players come in all colors, shapes, and sizes, but they are still overwhelmingly male. In this book, I'll continue to refer to chess players as *he*. Hopefully, the situation will someday be different.

I strongly recommend a detailed study of the material in these pages for any aspiring chess player. After all, as nice as it is to admire the artistic combinations that the great chess players have given us, it's much more satisfying to create them ourselves! And I hope this book will be the tool that allows you this satisfaction.

While you are studying tactics and combinations, you might find yourself spending long hours alone, huddled over your chessboard. As soon as you're ready, I advise you to get out and test your skills against those of other chess enthusiasts. Though reading this book will not guarantee that you'll win, it might start you on your way to a championship.

The sport of chess is remarkably well organized; in fact, very few sports have such a large international network of players. Local clubs, states, and national federations organize club championships, state championships, and national championships. A scoring system of 1 point for a victory, ½ point for a draw, and 0 points for a loss allows contestants to gradually attain Master, International Master and Grandmaster status. The 146 national federations, including the US Chess Federation, all belong to the Fédération Internationale des Échecs (FIDE), which organizes the World Championships. The World Championships are contested for millions of dollars; in fact, the prize fund for the 1993 World Championship match is $4 million!

So join your local club, enter and win tournaments, and who knows, you might manage to bag yourself a championship.

Happy hunting!

Yasser Seirawan
Seattle, Washington

PART 1

Tactics and Combinations

This part is the meat of the book. After defining tactics and combinations, I break them down into themes that I explain briefly before offering examples that illustrate the "how to" and "why." Most of these examples are fairly basic, but occasionally I throw in something more difficult to show how the simplest tactic can be combined with another and yet another to produce something mind-boggling.

If an example is not clear to you, go over it many times. If you continue to draw a blank, go over the section again and again and again until your raw, paper-cut fingers can't turn another page, your bloodshot eyes see only the hazy outlines of chess boards, and you begin to wish you had never taken up the sport of chess! (Hmmm. . . Perhaps I should get out of the chess business and start a new career as a drill sergeant!)

CHAPTER ONE

Definitions

I know, definitions are boring. You'd probably just as soon skip them and jump right into a few juicy games. Be patient. We'll get to the games—and some of them are beauties—soon enough. But before we delve into the world of tactics and combinations, we should begin by defining them. For some strange reason, these terms seem to cause confusion. Just what are tactics and combinations? Surprisingly, coming up with a satisfactory definition of these commonly used chess terms is more difficult than one might suppose.

Tactics

Chess is a game of *strategy* where two people pit their wits by mobilizing their pieces and developing plans based on such elements as force (the numerical value of the various pieces), time (the efficiency with which the pieces are developed), space (the territory controlled by each player), and pawn structure. Good players like to pick a strategy and follow it to its logical conclusion. Unfortunately, they're often thwarted by a strange randomizing factor known as *tactics*.

Tactics can both support your own strategy and destroy your opponent's strategy. They take the wind out of general strategic plans because they have the power to completely and advantageously change any situation. Thus, we arrive at this definition of tactics:

Tactics are maneuvers that take advantage of short-term opportunities.

For example, suppose your neighbor has invited you for dinner and an evening of chess. You've enjoyed a scrumptious banquet, and the game has been laced with heady amounts of port. Your neighbor must now face your guillotine. Under no circumstances do you want to lose. Your strategy is to control the center and prepare an inexorable Kingside assault. Who can argue with the principle of such an approach? However, in the middle of the plan, your opponent engineers a Knight fork that picks up one of your Rooks. You're busted, and your game falls apart. A brilliant strategy wrecked by a simple Knight fork. Where did you make your mistake? You are the victim of a tactic. Clearly, you have lots to learn.

Conversely, you can use tactics to your advantage. They can act as an early warning system that prevents your opponent from intruding on your plans with tricks of his own. As you work through the lessons in this book, you will come to realize that tactics are actually the guard dogs of strategy. By staying on top of the tactical possibilities, you will be able to defend yourself against your opponent's tactical forays and force him to follow the strategic path you want him to tread.

Combinations

In the classical chess literature, there has been tremendous disagreement as to the true meaning of the term *combination*. Surely the World Champion Emanuel Lasker (he enjoyed a 27-year reign—one of the longest in history) should know what a combination is! Let's take a look at his thoughts on the subject:

> In the rare instances in which the player can detect a variation, or set of variations, which leads to a desirable issue by force, the totality of these variations and their logical connections, their structure, are called a combination.

Lasker's definition has several problems, however. First, his style is ponderous and does not promote an easy understanding of the term. Second, he considers combinations to be rare occurrences, which is not at all the case. Combinations of some sort can be found in the *majority* of master games, sometimes in the moves actually played and often in the variations hidden behind those moves. Third, Lasker fails to mention that all combinations include a sacrifice. Fourth and perhaps most important, he claims that combinations necessarily lead to a "desirable issue by force," leaving out any possibility that a combination could fail and lead to the loss of the game. What about a situation in which you have a clear advantage, try a beautiful combinative idea, and after a perfect defense from your opponent, you find your advantage devalued to plain equality? Is an unsound combination no longer a combination simply because it is flawed? Certainly not!

This tendency to ignore the possibility of incorrect combinations also mars this otherwise excellent definition offered by former World Champion Mikhail Botvinnik:

> A combination is a forced maneuver or maneuvers combined with a sacri-
> fice as a result of which the active side gains an objective advantage.

Note Botvinnik's use of the word *sacrifice*. He is saying that the marriage of a forcing series of moves *with* a sacrifice makes a combination. This definition is easy to read and understand but falls short of the mark because of the final few words, "gains an objective advantage."

> Building on the efforts of these great men, I offer this simple definition:
> *A combination is a sacrifice combined with a forced sequence of moves,*
> *which exploits specific peculiarities of the position in the hope of*
> *attaining a certain goal.*

So we have managed to define the beast, but does this definition make it easier for you to recognize a combination? Not at all! To develop a feeling for combinations, we must break them down into types that you can familiarize yourself with. I discuss each type in detail in the chapters that follow.

Recognizing Tactics and Combinations

Two authors, Grandmaster Yuri Averbakh and International Master Jeremy Silman, have written extensively on tactics and combinations. Two books in particular, Averbakh's *Tactics for the Advanced Player* (Sporverlag Berlin, 1986) and Silman's *How to Reassess Your Chess* (Davenport: Thinkers' Press, 1986), suggest useful shortcuts that make it easier to recognize situations where tactics and combinations might exist. Let's look at some of these authors' theories.

Averbakh's Rules of Recognition

Averbakh considers that almost all combinations are based in some way on a double attack:

> If we regard the term "double attack" in a broader sense than has been done up to now by theoreticians, namely not merely as a two-pronged attack but as a combination of attacks and threats, we notice that the double attack in one form or another is the basis of most tactical operations.

At first I didn't want to agree with such a simplified view, but the more I thought about it, the more sensible Averbakh's theory sounded. The double attack is tremendously important, and I recommend that you spend a good deal of time going over the examples of double attacks in Chapter Two. Once you have mastered the material there and have moved on, you will notice that the combinations in later chapters also involve double attacks, which seems to confirm Averbakh's theory.

Silman's Rules of Recognition

Silman insists that combinations cannot exist without one or more of the following present:

■ A weakened (or open) King. When a King has poor pawn cover, has no defenders, or is otherwise weak, a combination is probably in the works.

■ A stalemated King. When a King has no legal moves, tactics that produce check also result in checkmate.

■ Undefended pieces (not pawns). Any unguarded piece is subject to destruction by a double attack or fork.

■ Inadequately guarded pieces. Such a piece appears to be safe, but a sudden double attack can place the piece in jeopardy by adding another attacker.

If you notice one or more of these factors on the board, Silman contends that you should look for a combination. However, if none of these factors is present, it is doubtful that a combination will materialize.

Well, that's it for the definitions. It wasn't so bad, was it? Now you need to train yourself to spot combinations. How do you do that? Learn the tactics presented in this book, gain a thorough understanding of the double attack theme, and practice Silman's Rules of Recognition. You will then be a very dangerous opponent!

CHAPTER TWO

The Double Attack

A double attack, as the name implies, is an attack against two pieces or pawns at the same time. Beginning players quickly learn that a simple attack against a single enemy piece or pawn can easily be countered in a variety of ways. A better alternative is a simultaneous attack against two pieces or pawns, only one of which can be defended by the opponent. This type of attack is the basis for much of the tactical play in chess.

Although some experts maintain that a double attack must involve two different pieces, I also consider forks (attacking two pieces or pawns with just one piece or pawn) to be double attacks. In this chapter, we'll take a look at three types of double attack:

■ Discovered attacks

■ Forks

■ Attacks by a pawn

The double attack is a tactic. It doesn't qualify as a combination for two reasons: First, a double attack can be one move as opposed to a series of moves; and second, a double attack doesn't necessarily involve a sacrifice. Many other tactical themes involve double attacks; these themes are studied in later chapters. Here, we'll look at the double attack in its purest forms.

Discovered Attacks

A discovered attack is essentially an ambush. Here's a general definition:

A Queen, Rook, or Bishop lies in wait so that it can attack when another piece or pawn of its own color moves out of its way.

Let's look at some examples.

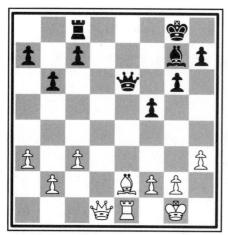

DIAGRAM 1. White to play.

DIAGRAM 2. White to play.

Diagram 1 shows a simple but clear example of a discovered attack. If White moves his Bishop, he will create a discovered attack on the Black Queen with the Rook on e1. However, moves like 1.Bd3 or 1.Bf3 don't accomplish much because Black would sidestep his Queen to safety on d6 or f6. This is where the double attack comes in handy. By playing **1.Ba6!**, White creates a discovered attack on Black's Queen and also attacks his Rook on c8, threatening two pieces at once with one move.

After you have grasped the principle in an example, it can be instructive to change the position a bit to see how the change affects the result. In Diagram 1, how would putting the Black b6-pawn on b7 affect the situation? What if the Black Rook were on a8 instead of c8?

In Diagram 2, Black has two Knights (6 points) vs. a Rook and a pawn (6 points) and appears to be doing well. Unfortunately, both Knights are undefended. (Remember Silman's Rules of Recognition from Chapter One.) White creates a discovered attack with **1.Ke3!**. Suddenly Black's d8-Knight is attacked by White's Rook, and the f3-Knight is threatened by White's King. Black, to his sorrow, is forced to part with a Knight.

As in Diagram 1, White has the chance in Diagram 3 to initiate a discovered attack on the Black Queen by moving his Bishop out of the way

10

of his Rook. Quiet moves like 1.Be3 or 1.Bc3 don't take advantage of the situation (no double attack!) because Black would calmly move his Queen to safety with 1...Qe8 or 1...Qf8. However, White can attack both the Queen and the Bishop on e7 with the surprising **1.Bg5!** (1.Bb4! accomplishes the same thing). Normally such a move is impossible because the Bishop is hanging to both the h6-pawn and the Bishop on e7, but in this case the discovered attack

DIAGRAM 3. **White to play.**

on Black's Queen by the Rook makes the Bishop a less attractive tidbit. After **1.Bg5!**, Black has to make a difficult choice. He could move his Queen to safety with 1...Qe8, but then the point of 1.Bg5 would be obvious: White would be attacking the Bishop on e7 with both his Queen and his Bishop while Black would be defending his Bishop only once with his Queen. Then, with the simple 2.Bxe7, White would pick up a piece for free (a gain of 3 points). Although most players hate to part with their Queen, a much better move for Black is **1...Bxg5! 2.Rxd8+ Rxd8.** True, Black loses his Queen (9 points). But in return, he gains a Rook and a Bishop (for a total of 8 points). He is down only 1 point and can still put up a tough fight.

There is another possibility in the position. (Always remember the words of the great Emanuel Lasker: "When you see a good move, look for a better one!" Sound advice. Inexperienced players have a tendency to make the first move that looks good.) Instead of the strong 1.Bg5!, White might also consider 1.Bxh6! This move wins a pawn (1 point) because the Bishop is invulnerable due to the discovered attack on Black's Queen. This alternative is an example of a pure discovered attack. It is not a double attack because only one Black piece (the Queen) is threatened.

DIAGRAM 4. White to play.

The position in Diagram 4 is identical to that in Diagram 3 with two exceptions: White's Queen sits on f3 instead of e2, and Black's Rook sits on b8 instead of a8. Is 1.Bg5 or 1.Bb4 still a good move? No! Black is now able to step out of harm's way with 1...Qf8 because 2.Bxe7 Qxe7 leads only to an even trade of pieces. The big difference between this and the previous diagram is a result of the White Queen's position on e2. Previously she joined in the attack against the Bishop on e7. Because 1.Bg5 now fails to yield any advantage, White is better off playing either 1.Bxh6, which wins a pawn, or the stronger 1.Bf4!, which creates a discovered attack on the Queen and an additional attack on Black's Rook on b8. After **1.Bf4! Qf8 2.Bxb8 Qxb8**, White ends up winning an Exchange—a Rook for a Bishop or Knight—for a 2-point advantage.

Discovered Checks

The most effective type of discovered attack involves *checking the enemy King*. This type of discovered attack is even stronger if it includes a double attack. Because of the check, the opponent is helpless to prevent the other attacking piece or pawn from devouring its victim. Let's look at a few examples of discovered checks.

If we do nothing but count points, the position in Diagram 5 appears to be very good for Black. His Queen (9 points) outguns White's Bishop on a1 (3 points). However, instead of counting points, look carefully at the position. When White attacks the Black Queen with **1.Ne4+**, Black can't move his Queen to safety because White's move also unleashes a discovered

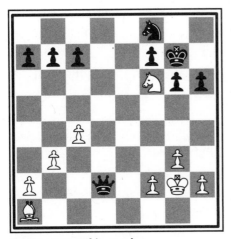

DIAGRAM 5. White to play.

DIAGRAM 6. White to play.

attack by the White Bishop against the Black King. This discovered check is Black's doom. He must get out of check with **1...Kg8**, whereupon White calmly eats the Black Queen with **2.Nxd2**. White now has an extra piece and a commanding 3-point advantage.

Diagram 6 shows another example of a crushing discovered check attack. White plays the kamikaze **1.Bh7+!**, checking the Black King and uncovering the Rook, which now threatens the Black Queen. Black would dearly love to take the unprotected White Rook with 1...Qxd1+, but the rules won't let him leave his King in check. Poor Black is forced to play **1...Kxh7**, after which **2.Rxd6** picks up the Black Queen and gives White a material advantage.

By now you probably realize that it is not a good idea to leave your Queen opposite a Rook, no matter how many pieces are between them!

One of the guiding strategic principles of chess is

When you are ahead in material, it is a good idea to make even trades.
Why? Because as the number of pieces you have on the board decreases, the relative importance of a material advantage—even of only a pawn—increases.

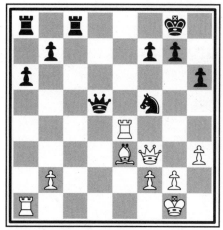

DIAGRAM 7. Black to play.

For example, in Diagram 7, Black is a pawn ahead and would like to exchange pieces. In his attempt to force an ending without Queens, Black plays **1...Nd6**. Is this a good move? By attacking White's Rook, Black hopes, after something like 2.Rf4 or 2.Re7, to exchange Queens. Unfortunately for Black, 1...Nd6?? is a blunder! He has forgotten that his Queen is completely undefended. (Remember Silman's Rules of Recognition!) With **2.Re8+!**, White places his Rook on a hopeless square, but thereby allows the White Queen to uncover an attack on its counterpart on d5. Black must get out of check, but after he captures the offensive Rook with **2...Nxe8** or **2...Rxe8**, White snaps off the Black Queen with **3.Qxd5**, for a hefty 3-point material advantage (9 for the Queen vs. 5 for the Rook plus 1 for the extra pawn).

Was Black wrong to want to trade pieces? No, but he went about it in an unfortunate way. The correct route is the simple **1...Nxe3!** because then 2.Qxe3 will leave Black with a solid extra pawn. Note that White's discovered check tactic no longer works. To **2.Re8+??**, Black responds with **2...Rxe8**. Then **3.Qxd5** fails to **3...Nxd5** because the Knight on e3 is protecting Black's Queen. According to an eloquent old friend of mine, the moral of this story is

Don't leave your stuff unprotected. It might get chopped off!

It's important to note that the seven board positions we've looked at so far are simple illustrations of a tactical theme. Diagrams 6 and 7 also offer us our first glimpses of combinations. In Diagram 7, we saw a sacrifice— 2.Re8+!—that led to a forced response. Black had to get out of check, so White achieved his goal of capturing the undefended enemy Queen.

Double Checks

The most powerful type of discovered attack is the *double check*. This type of check tends to be very strong because it checks the King with two pieces. The King is forced to move, and the enemy army is thus frozen for at least one move.

In Diagram 8, White is a pawn ahead, but appears to be on the verge of defeat because his Rook is pinned by the Black Bishop. After Black captures White's Rook, Black will be the one with the edge in material. White's solution to the pin is **1.Bd6++!**—a double check. (Don't forget that a pinned piece is still able to check!) Black would love to capture the Rook or Bishop, but his King is being attacked by two pieces, and he can't chop off both the offenders at the same time. Black's best reply is **1...Kg8**. Then **2.Bxc5** breaks the pin and leaves White with an extra piece and pawn.

Diagram 9 is a silly but graphic example of a discovered attack turned into a double check. Black is so far ahead in material that one would expect White to give up and do something more enjoyable with his time. However, instead of resigning, White plays **1.Ng6++**, and wonder of wonders... the move produces double check and mate!

DIAGRAM 8. White to play.

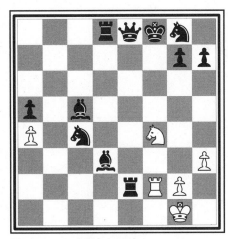

DIAGRAM 9. White to play.

Now that you understand the basics of discovered attacks and double checks, I'll give you the opportunity to try to figure out some tactics on your own. The first few tests in the next section will be reasonably easy, but they will get harder. In fact, some of them are very hard. Don't get discouraged if you don't get all the answers! Instead, just relax, do your best, and study the solutions given in Chapter Twenty-Four.

Tests

TEST 1. It's Black's move. White has given Black the chance to capture his pawn on g2 with 1...Rxg2. Is this a trap? Should Black munch the g2-pawn?

TEST 2. With material even in a boring endgame, this game seems destined for a draw. But tactics can be used in the most innocent settings. It's White's turn to play. Can he win material?

TEST 3. Black's game appears to be fine. He has plenty of space for his army, the Black Bishop is more active than its counterpart, and the Black passed pawn on d4 is solidly defended. It's White's turn to play. How can he turn the tables?

TEST 4. It's White's move. His Bishop is pinned—if it moves, White's Rook will fall prey to Black's Queen—and his Rook is attacked by the Bishop on f6. As a result, Black is feeling pretty good about himself. It seems that White's best chance is 1.Rd1 c6 2.Bb3 Qxd1+ 3.Qxd1 Rxd1+ 4.Bxd1 Bxb2, leaving Black with an extra pawn for the ending. Can you find anything better for White?

TEST 5. It's White's turn to play. Black's Queen and Rook are putting formidable pressure on the e-file. White must worry about the e3-pawn being swallowed with check and then a Black Knight sinking into the fine e4-square. Can you find the White move that throws these positional considerations out the window?

TEST 6. As I mentioned, tactics and combinations are the foundation of classical chess play. I had to rummage through the dustier parts of my library for this position, which is the conclusion of a study by a gifted chess "composer," A. Troitzky, in 1896! (Studies are compositions that highlight unusual tactical themes.) In this study, White has an extra pawn and is one step away from queening. Unfortunately, his Rook is in the way, and any move by the Rook will allow Black to capture the pawn with ...Rxa7. If White tries 1.Kb6, protecting the pawn and threatening to move the Rook, Black will chase the White King away with 1...Rb1+ 2.Kc7 Ra1, putting White back in the same unfortunate situation. Can White win by creating a discovered check?

TEST 7. This position is taken from a correspondence game played in 1952–53 between Dunhaupt and Kunert. (In correspondence chess, the players play by mail, exchanging a move every two weeks. Some games take years! Imagine playing a game for three years and losing. Ouch!) It's White's move. His Bishop blocks his Rook on d7 from attacking the f7-pawn. However, most Bishop moves allow Black to cover the f7-pawn by retreating with 1...Qf5. Can you find a way to use a discovered attack against the f7-pawn to finish off Black?

TEST 8. White's Bishops are bearing down on the Black King. The Bishop on b2 is doing a wonderful job of pinning the Knight on f6. Black is willing to suffer this pin because he is up a piece for two pawns. Furthermore, Black is cheered by the fact that White's Rook is pinned and is about to be eaten by the Bishop on g4. It's White's turn to play. How can he put both of his Bishops to work?

Forks

Forks are tactical maneuvers in which a piece or pawn attacks two enemy pieces or pawns at the same time. Many beginners think that only Knights can accomplish forks. But in fact other pieces, including the King, are capable of attacking two enemy men at the same time.

In this section, we'll look at how each *piece* can create a fork. In a later section, I'll show you how pawns can create forks. Let's start with the dreaded Knights!

Knight Forks

Most beginning chess players live in fear of the enemy Knights. However, if you take the time to study the Knight's eccentric way of moving, you will notice that the Knight can never attack squares of two different colors at the same time. This knowledge can sometimes come in handy when you are choosing where to put your men in the face of Knight threats.

Because of the Knight's unusual way of hopping around the board, beginners are often taken by surprise and find themselves the victim of a Knight fork. Here are some examples.

In Diagram 10, the force count is even, but White changes the situation dramatically with **1.Nc7+**, forking both the King and the Rook. Black must move his King, which allows **2.Nxa8** and puts White ahead by a whole Rook.

The position in Diagram 11 revolves around the same theme. With **1.Nc7+**, White attacks no less than four Black pieces—both Rooks, the King, and the Queen—at the same time! (A fork that attacks the King and the Queen is called a *royal fork*.) I've been the victim of this often enough. When it happens to you, don't become "Knight phobic." Instead, consider it a lesson well learned and be sure in the future to defend yourself against such possibilities.

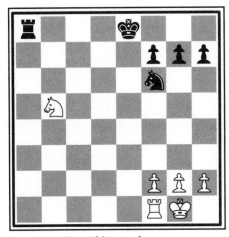

DIAGRAM 10. White to play.

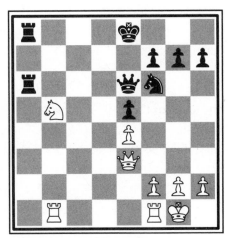

DIAGRAM 11. White to play.

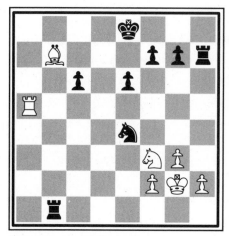

DIAGRAM 12. White to play.

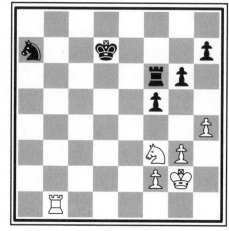

DIAGRAM 13. White to play.

Bishop Forks

In Diagram 12, Black has a material advantage, but it proves to be short-lived. With **1.Bxc6+**, White creates a fork—a double attack on both the Black King and Knight. After **1...Ke7 2.Bxe4**, Black thinks he has recovered satisfactorily because he is only down 1 point—two minor pieces (6 points) vs. one Rook (5 points). But to his horror he notices that a new fork has been created! Now his Rooks on b1 and h7 are both under attack, and one must be lost. This second fork shows that a fork does not always involve a check: All pieces are vulnerable.

Rook Forks

In Diagram 13, White shows that he knows how to use his Rook to fork with **1.Rb7+**. After **1...Kc6 2.Rxa7**, the Rook has gobbled a Knight. White's material advantage should lead to an easy victory.

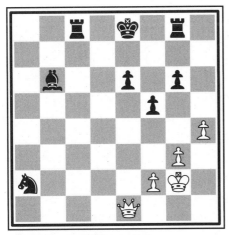

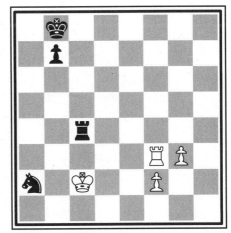

DIAGRAM 14. White to play.   DIAGRAM 15. White to play.

Queen Forks

Because the Queen moves like a Rook and a Bishop, it stands to reason that the Queen can fork like either of these pieces, with even greater effect. From the position in Diagram 14, the White Queen will show her power and terrorize the whole Black army. White attacks with **1.Qxe6+ Kf8** (no better is 1...Kd8 2.Qxg8+ Kc7.3.Qxa2) **2.Qxc8+** (this Rook is the fork's first payoff) **2...Kg7.** With **3.Qb7+,** White creates a new fork that will add the Bishop to the Queen's feast. After **3...Kh6 4.Qxb6,** White enjoys a 2-point advantage—the Queen and a pawn (10 points) vs. a Rook and a Knight (8 points).

King Forks

In Diagram 15, Black is attacking the White Monarch, so the King must move to get out of check. The interposition, 1.Rc3??, would lose the Rook. However, White can turn the tables with **1.Kb3!,** by which the White King changes from the hunted to the hunter. This fork means the certain capture of either Black's Knight or Rook. Black would be well advised to save his more valuable Rook. As this example shows, even the stately King can fork other hapless pieces.

Forks as Combinations

Now that you understand the fork as a tactic, we can take the next step and see how this tactic can be changed into a combination. In Diagram 16, White can take advantage of Black's unprotected Bishop and his checkable King. With **1.Qc2+**, White wins the Bishop on c6, because Black must get his King out of check before he can do anything else.

Nice and simple. Let's increase the difficulty level a bit with the position in Diagram 17, which is similar to the one in Diagram 16. Here, Black's Bishop is still unprotected on c6, but this time his King is safer. White could try for a fork with 1.Qc2, creating a double attack on g6 and c6. However, Black could then defend himself with either 1...Qe8, which guards both c6 and g6, or the retreat 1...Be8. Clearly, White needs to take a more forceful approach. The correct move is **1.Bxg6+!**, whereby White sacrifices a piece to create the position in Diagram 16. (The important word here is *create*. A good player doesn't just sit around and hope that a tactic will materialize; he uses every means at his disposal to make it happen.) Black now faces a decision. If he doesn't take White's Bishop, it will retreat to safety, having enjoyed its pawn snack. After **1...Kxg6 2.Qc2+**, Black loses his Bishop on c6 and ends up down one pawn in the Queen ending.

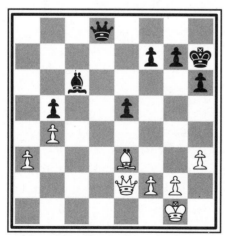

DIAGRAM 16. White to play.

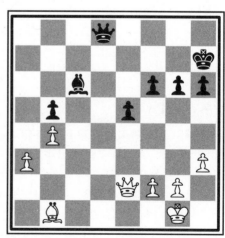

DIAGRAM 17. White to play.

This example of a sacrifice to gain a pawn is known as a *petite combinaison* (a small combination) because it involves only three moves. But some combinations involve over a dozen moves and feature many types of tactics. (We'll discuss these *grandes combinaisons* later.) Though the body of knowledge that we call "chess theory" has made tremendous strides in the last 100 years, the nature of combinations has remained essentially the same. The one area in which players of the 19th century were the equals of modern-day masters is in combinative play, because imagination and calculating ability, rather than theoretical knowledge, hold sway in the kingdom of combinations.

Now take a look at Diagrams 18 and 19. In Diagram 18, a simple Knight fork with **1.Nc7+ Kd7 2.Nxd5** leads to the capture of a pawn, whereas in Diagram 19, Black's Queen defends the c7-square, preventing a Knight fork. However, White can use a common sacrifice to draw the Black Queen away from c7 and allow the fork to take place after all. White begins with **1.Qxd5!** **Qxd5** (leaving c7 undefended) **2.Nc7+** (creating a royal fork) **2...Kd7** **3.Nxd5**. White regains his Queen with a one-pawn advantage.

Now compare Diagrams 18 and 19 again. Why was the position in Diagram 18 easier to play than the one in Diagram 19? The reason is mostly psychological. We've been taught not to give the Queen away, and our

DIAGRAM 18. White to play.

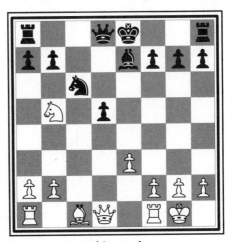

DIAGRAM 19. White to play.

minds clamp shut rather than consider the possibility of sacrificing this valuable piece. Does this reluctance to sacrifice mean that you will never master combinations? Will you have to go through hours of brainwashing or hypnosis to break down these mental barriers? Of course not! A large part of chess skill is pattern recognition, and as you become more acquainted with the basic tactical forms, you'll find it easier to create combinations. The trick is to isolate and understand the various types of tactics. Only then will you be able to put them all together to razzle-dazzle your stunned opponent.

Here's another example. In Diagram 20, Black is down a pawn, but he has been counting on this position to bring him victory. Triumphantly playing **1...Nxb3**, he looks his opponent in the eye and flashes a winner's smile. The move certainly looks powerful. Not only does it win back the pawn, but Black's Knight now forks White's Rooks. Unfortunately for Black, the move is actually awful. White calmly slides his Bishop to the middle of the board with **2.Bd5+**, after which it becomes apparent that Black has walked into a more potent fork! Black's smile turns to a frown, and he hangs his head in resignation. He has to lose his Knight because getting out of check overrides all other considerations.

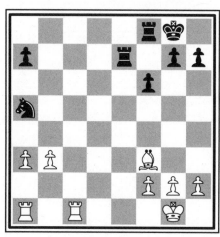

DIAGRAM 20. **Black to play.**

Imagine that the sad loser of the position in Diagram 20 was stung by the reversal he suffered in that game. He was a good student of chess, though, and he made a point of never falling into the same trap twice. A few weeks later, he is faced with the position in Diagram 21 and has another chance to chop off a b3-pawn. Feeling very wise, he notes that 1...Rxb3 would be a terrible blunder because of 2.Bd5+. However, the simple 1...Nxb3 seems safe enough because the Rook on d3 prevents the rude White Bishop from checking on d5. Again he confidently plays **1...Nxb3??**, and again he is treated to a quick dose of harsh reality. After **2.Rxb3! Rxb3 3.Bd5+**, he can only stare in horror. That brutal Bishop appears to have a personal grudge against him! When White captures the Black Rook on the next move, Black resigns the game because he's now down a piece for a pawn (2 points).

DIAGRAM 21. Black to play.

Let's compare two more positions. In Diagram 22, White forks the King and a pawn with **1.Rg5+**, and then **2.Rxg4** snags the pawn. The position in Diagram 23 is identical to that of Diagram 22, with the addition of the Knights. This addition seems to make Black's life easier, because the White Rook's access to g5 is blocked, and Black's Knight defends the g4-pawn. However, Easy Street is just an illusion, because **1.Nxg4!** allows White his big check on g5. After **1...Nxg4 2.Rg5+ Kf8 3.Rxg4**, Black loses a pawn.

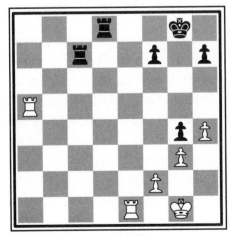

DIAGRAM 22. White to play.

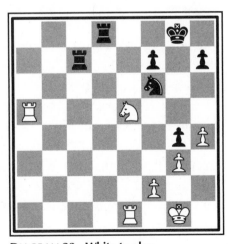

DIAGRAM 23. White to play.

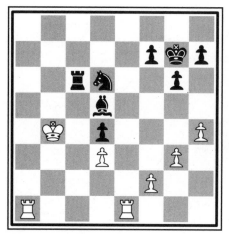

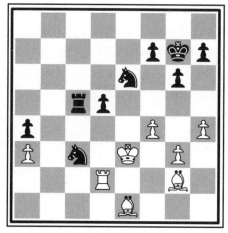

DIAGRAM 24. Black to play.   DIAGRAM 25. Black to play.

In Diagram 24, Black's pieces are hounding White's King, but Black commits a cardinal sin. With **1...Rb6+??**, he makes a check without considering the consequences. (The simple 1...Rc3 would have been a stronger move.) White's King shows its muscle with **2.Kc5!** and makes contact with all of Black's attacking pieces. Black is forced to give up either his Rook, Knight, or Bishop, and he goes on to lose the game.

This game teaches an important lesson:

Never check just because you can. Be sure that you gain from making a check, not your opponent.

America's former World Champion, Robert Fischer, once made a premature check that spoiled a beautiful position that had taken him hours to create. Afterwards he coined the phrase, "Patzer sees check, patzer gives check!"

Here's one more example of a fork. In Diagram 25, Black is a pawn up, but the position is still tricky. Hoping to use his extra pawn, Black plays **1...d4+?**, thinking that this will place his d-pawn on a safer square while defending his Knight on c3. White's reply comes as a shock: **2.Rxd4! Nxd4 3.Kxd4**. Suddenly, White's King attacks Black's Rook, while two White pieces, the King and the Bishop on e1, go after Black's Knight. Black is forced to part with another piece, giving White an advantage in material.

26

Now try some tests that involve forks. As usual, I'll start with easy positions and then gradually increase the level of difficulty. Good luck.

Tests

TEST 9. It's White's turn to play. He is tempted to grab the a4-pawn. Is this the best move?

TEST 10. White has two things going for him: the possibility of a fork on e7, currently prevented by the Black Rook on c7, and pressure against Black's c6-pawn. Does White have any way to make these advantages bear fruit?

TEST 11. It's White's move. Here he has a problem similar to that of the previous test. How would you take advantage of this position?

Seirawan–Costigan
US Open, 1977

TEST 12. This position is taken from one of my own games. It's my move and I'm up two pawns, but Black hopes to pick up one of my White Rooks for his Bishop. Fortunately for me, Black's King is very weak and his Bishop on a3 is not defended. How did I take advantage of these two factors?

Seirawan–Hessen
Seattle, 1975

TEST 13. Another fond memory from my tournament career. It's my move and material is even, but that undefended Knight on d7 gives me a chance that I am quick to take. What did I play?

Lipschütz–Schallopp
London, 1886

TEST 14. It's White's turn to play. This position is a really tough one for him. Can you find the beautiful solution?

TEST 15. It's Black's turn to play. He doesn't seem to have any fork possibilities here. Can you create one?

Tolush–Simagin
USSR, 1952

TEST 16. This position occurred in a game I played in my first US Championship. Texas Joe Bradford is known as a tough man to beat. He has good central control and enjoys more space than I do. I'm Black, and it's my move. How was I able to take advantage of the undefended White Bishop on c4?

Bradford–Seirawan
US Championship, 1980

Double Attacks by a Pawn

Pawns are one of the paradoxes of chess: The fact that pawns are considered weak makes the much-stronger minor pieces and the major pieces fear them. You don't believe me? To support my argument, let's take a look at one of history's shortest master games.

H. Borochow–R. Fine
Pasadena, 1932

Who would guess that the player handling the Black pieces, Reuben Fine, would become one of the world's greatest chess masters? Remember, good players become good only after suffering lots of defeats. So take heart!

1.e4 Nf6

Chess has been played for centuries, and records have been kept of the strongest players' games. Over the years, opening schemes that have stood the test of time have been given names. Openings have been named for the nationality of players who championed their cause (Russian Defense, French Defense, English Opening, and so forth) or for the place where games featuring that opening were played (Merano Defense, Cambridge Springs Defense, Catalan Opening, and so on). However, the most common practice is to name an opening for the individual who introduced the scheme into tournament play. After a millenium of chess games, entire encyclopedias are now devoted to cataloging all the various openings! Black's first move, 1...Nf6 in response to 1.e4 by White, is known as Alekhine's Defense, in deference to former World Champion Alexander Alekhine, who invented this opening. Black's strategy is to allow White to push his center pawns, hoping that they will become overextended and turn into targets. The strategy is a risky one.

2.e5

The first example of the pawn's power: The little guy tells the mighty Knight to scram. The Knight has no choice but to do as it's bidden, evidence of the pawn paradox. The more valuable pieces cannot allow themselves to be traded for a lowly pawn, so they must run from its slightest threat!

2...Nd5

3.c4

White continues to kick the poor beast around.

3...Nb6

4.d4 Nc6??

A blunder. Black should have challenged White's center with 4...d6, which would be the main line of Alekhine's Defense.

5.d5!

So it's a battle between Black's Knights and White's pawns. The mighty steeds don't stand a chance!

5...Nxe5

Black would also lose after 5...Nb4 6.c5 N6xd5 7.a3, with which White wins a Knight.

6.c5 Nbc4

The slap-happy Knight has nowhere to run, so it's forced to step forward to its doom.

7.f4

After several more moves, Black resigns.

Now that we have seen the pawns in action, we can take a look at their virtues:

- ■ You have more of them than of any other piece.

- ■ They are "baby Queens." Each has the potential to become a Queen when it reaches the other side of the board.

- ■ If you trade a pawn for a piece, you get the better part of the deal.

Pawn Forks

Armed with this theoretical knowledge, let's jump right into some practical examples of pawn forks. In Diagram 26, Black should play 1...dxe4 or 1...Bb4, but instead he makes a typical beginner's mistake: **1...Bd6?? 2.e5!** This pawn fork will win one of the Black pieces. Amazing, but true: The two mighty Black pieces are helpless against the lowly White pawn!

DIAGRAM 26. Black to play.

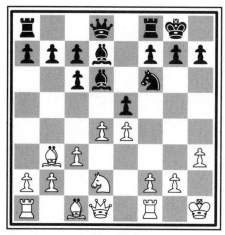 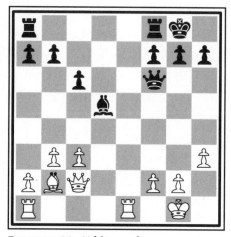

DIAGRAM 27. White to play.   DIAGRAM 28. White to play.

By creating a pawn fork in Diagram 27, White has two ways of winning material. One method is **1.f4!**, by which White threatens to play 2.fxe5, thereby winning a pawn and forking two Black pieces. If Black answers with either **1...exf4** or **1...exd4**, then **2.e5** leads to the desired fork. The other possibility is **1.dxe5! Bxe5 2.f4**, which threatens Black's Bishop. The cleric's only retreat, **2...Bd6**, is smashed by **3.e5** and another fork.

These examples make it clear that pawns are a menace. If you can't completely eradicate the critters, you must respectfully tiptoe around them. Don't make them mad: They obviously bite!

Discovered Attacks with Pawns

Aside from forking, pawns can also take part in discovered attacks. As shown in Diagram 28, White can create a discovered attack with **1.c4**. White's Bishop on b2 suddenly threatens Black's Queen, while Black's Bishop on d5 is ambushed by the pawn. Black loses material.

Tests

TEST 17. It's Black's turn to play. Would 1...Qg5 be a reasonable move?

TEST 18. It's White's move. Black's position seems to be secure, but he is actually set up for a knockout punch. Can you find a *petite combination* that allows White to create a pawn fork?

TEST 19. White has a Rook and two pawns for two Knights, a 7-points to 6-points material advantage. However, the d6-pawn is threatened by Black's Knight on e8. It's White's turn to play. Although White could defend the pawn by playing 1.Rcd1, he could instead force a sequence of moves that features the tactics I've shown. Can you find the second solution? Frustration alert! This problem isn't easy!

Kikovic–Forintos
Budapest, 1957

CHAPTER THREE

The Pin

When you attack a piece that your opponent cannot move without losing a different piece of greater value, you are *pinning* the first piece. When the piece of greater value is the King, this tactic is called an *absolute pin*; when it is not the King, the tactic is called a *relative pin*. Clearly an absolute pin is a far more serious threat than a relative pin because your opponent absolutely cannot move the pinned piece. (Putting his own King in check is illegal.)

The pin is one of the most common tactics used in chess, so you should study it very carefully. Bear in mind that any piece is vulnerable to a pin, but only a Queen, Bishop, or Rook can do the pinning—a King, Knight, or pawn can only play the victim. Let's look at the absolute pin first.

Absolute Pins

Pins occur during all phases of the game, but they are most common in the opening. An example of a typical absolute pin in the opening is as follows: **1.e4 e5 2.Nf3 Nc6 3. Nc3 d6 4.Bb5**. The result is shown in Diagram 29. Black's Knight on c6 can't move because White's Bishop would then attack Black's King. Should Black panic at the first sign of such a pin? No, the Knight is well protected by the b7-pawn, and its capture by the White Bishop would

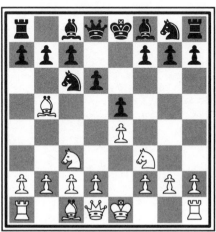

DIAGRAM 29. **Black to play.**

35

simply lead to an even trade. Because of this, Black can play **4...a6**, asking White what he intends to do with his Bishop. White then has to decide whether to trade pieces with **5.Bxc6+ bxc6** or to retreat with **5.Ba4** and allow Black to break the pin with **5...b5**.

If Black doesn't want to weaken his Queenside pawns, he would be wiser to play 4...Bd7 instead. This move gives the Knight an extra defender and simultaneously breaks the pin.

Although this particular pin does not prove to be fearsome, an absolute pin can have a powerful impact on many positions. Pins are particularly useful in fixing a piece on a vulnerable square so that it can be won at your leisure. Pins can also prevent a piece from taking part in an offensive or defensive maneuver elsewhere on the board.

Diagram 30 picks up the previous example where we left it. White has played the useful move d2–d4. Black has squandered a move with the awful a7–a5 and has lost the important a7–a6/b7–b5 pin-breaking possibility. Taking advantage of the situation, White now plays **1.d5**. The poor Black Knight is unable to run away from the pawn, and White wins a piece. It's that simple. Don't let a pin freeze your pieces on doomed squares.

Here's another opening sequence that commonly occurs in the games of beginners: **1.e4 d5 2.exd5 Qxd5**. Black's first two moves are known as the Scandinavian Defense. It is not a good choice for an opening. (Developing your Queen too early in the opening is very dangerous because enemy pieces can then develop with gain of tempo by attacking her.) White plays **3.Nc3**, the first gain. Black, who must move his Queen and avoid the horse's kick, plays **3...Qc6??**, a rotten move. (Best would have been 3...Qa5, which leaves

DIAGRAM 30. White to play.

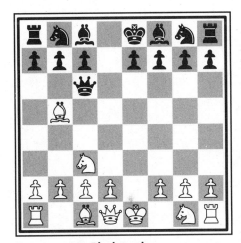

DIAGRAM 31. Black to play.

DIAGRAM 32. Black to play.

White with only a small opening advantage.) White responds with **4.Bb5!**, and the position is now as shown in Diagram 31.

It's only the fourth move, but Black has already lost his Queen, which is attacked by the Bishop. Playing 4...Qxb5 allows 5.Nxb5, but Black can't move his Queen to safety because it is pinned to his King. Black has no choice but to accept the loss of his most powerful piece for a mere Bishop (9 points for 3 points). A devastating absolute pin.

Black has a good position in Diagram 32, but is faced with temptation. Should he capture the hanging White Knight on e5? A snack of a free piece worth 3 points is always desirable. However, the answer in this case is a resounding No! Playing **1...Qxe5?** loses the Black Queen after **2.Re1**, because the Queen is pinned to her King. The moral:

Look carefully before you take any "free" gifts from your opponent. He may have prepared a clever trap!

You might have noticed that pins can be executed only by straight-line pieces (Queens, Rooks, and Bishops). Because of this, you should always be careful about putting vulnerable targets on the same line. Conversely, when your opponent puts potential targets on the same line, look for pins!

Experienced players develop a real sensitivity for this kind of mistake. For example, one of the first things a master would notice about the position

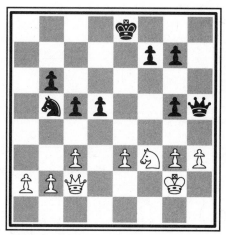

DIAGRAM 33. White to play.

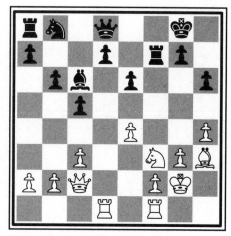

DIAGRAM 34. White to play.

shown in Diagram 33 is that Black's Knight and King are both on the a4–e8 line. White's Queen can show her pinning powers with **1.Qa4!**. Black's Knight is then pinned to his King, and no Black piece can defend it.

The position in Diagram 34 illustrates how one pin can lead to another. White plays **1.Bxe6!**, pinning the Rook on f7 to the Black King—an absolute pin. Black would like to take this impudent Bishop prisoner, but his d7-pawn is caught in a relative pin by White's Rook on d1. Black plays **1...dxe6**, whereupon **2.Rxd8+** wins the Black Queen. Black has fallen victim to a pin.

Let's make sure you've understood everything. The following tests feature pins, though I might have thrown in a ringer that features a fork.

Tests

TEST 20. It's White's turn to play. Black is pouring the pressure on White's center. How can White use an absolute pin to get to Black's King?

TEST 21. In this game, I defeated the Norwegian Junior Champion and was able to go on and win the World Junior Championship. I'm White, and it's my move. I have to create a situation that will lead to an absolute pin. What did I play?

Seirawan–Wiedenheller
Norway, 1979

TEST 22. It's White's move. He is in check and has to decide between two reasonable possibilities: 1.Kh1 and 1.Bd4. Which is the correct choice?

TEST 23. Here, Black interposed the check with 1...Qd4, offering a trade of Queens. Was this the best way to get out of check?

Stahlberg–Lundin

TEST 24. A tricky moment for White. He creates a fork possibility by utilizing an absolute pin. How did he do it?

Ed. Lasker–Aualla
New York, 1947

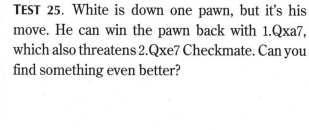

TEST 25. White is down one pawn, but it's his move. He can win the pawn back with 1.Qxa7, which also threatens 2.Qxe7 Checkmate. Can you find something even better?

TEST 26. Although material is even, Black has been tormented by White's advanced f6-pawn. It's Black's turn to play. Noticing that White's Bishop is in an absolute pin, Black takes the opportunity to play 1...Qxf6. Is this a good idea?

Relative Pins

Relative pins, in one form or another, come about in most games. For example, **1.e4 c6 2.Nc3 d5 3.Nf3 Bg4** produces a relative pin when the Black Bishop pins the White Knight to the White Queen. Then after **4.d4 e6 5.e5 Bb4**, we have an absolute pin. The difference between the two pins is that White can move the Knight on f3 (though he would have to accept the loss of his Queen after ...Bxd1). However, he can't move the Knight on c3. This Knight's inability to move isn't a matter of taste or desire; it's simply illegal. You cannot give your King away!

In Diagram 35, White is applying pressure on Black's c5-pawn, but the pawn is protected and everything seems to be under control. White proves otherwise and plays **Nxb4!** to take advantage of the pin on the g1–a7 diagonal and win a pawn. This relative pin is fairly common. Black could capture on b4, but White's reply of Bxb6 would only make matters worse.

Obviously, a relative pin is not as lethal as an absolute pin, so don't be surprised if the pinned piece moves. For a good example of a relative pin gone bad, let's look at a famous position from Philidor. After **1.e4 e5 2.Nf3 d6 3.Nc3 a6?** (a horrible waste of time) and **4.Bc4 Bg4??**, Black has pinned White's Knight as shown in Diagram 36 and is secure in the

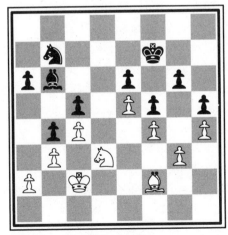

DIAGRAM 35. White to play.

DIAGRAM 36. White to play.

DIAGRAM 37. White to play.

DIAGRAM 38. Black to play.

knowledge that the horse is not going anywhere. However, he's in for a rude awakening. White plays **5.Nxe5!!**, breaking the pin but exposing the White Queen to danger. If Black takes the Knight with 5...dxe5, then 6.Qxg4 wins a clean pawn. Undaunted, Black goes for the big meal: **...Bxd1? 6.Bxf7+ Ke7 7.Nd5** Checkmate. Black won the Queen but lost his King.

From this example, it's clear that the hold of the relative pin cannot be taken for granted. Never assume that the pinned piece won't move.

The relative pin is most successful when an important piece is immediately threatened. Diagram 37 illustrates such an attack. Black's Knight on c6 is pinned because his Rook on a8 sits on the same diagonal as White's g2-Bishop. White has to take advantage of this opportunity; otherwise, Black will play ...Rad8, and the pin will no longer exist. White plays **1.b5**, attacking the c6-Knight. Rather than lose the Knight, Black will do best to move it to safety with **1...Ne7** and allow **2.Bxa8**, because then **2...Rxa8** leaves Black down only the Exchange. A loss of 2 points is much better than the 3-point deficit that results from the capture of the Knight.

Another advantage of the pinning tactic comes about when the defending player is unable to break the pin. He is then stuck nursing the pinned piece and must meekly wait for more pressure to be applied. For example, in Diagram 38, Black would love to move his Knight to safety with 1...Nd7, but because of the pin, 2.Bxd8 would lop off his Queen if he did so. A Queen move like 1...Qc7 simply hangs the Knight, so Black tries to give the horse extra support with **1...Kg7**. With this move, he hopes to gain the time to play 2...Qc7 followed by a Knight retreat of 3...Nd7 or 3...Ng8, which will break the pin. Being careful not to let Black off the hook, White increases the pressure with **2.Qh4** (2.Qc3, with an absolute pin on the a1–h8 diagonal, is also very strong). Black is then completely helpless to prevent **3.Rf1** followed by **4.Bxf6**, which captures the pinned Knight. This example shows why pins are to be feared!

Remember, when a pin is working, look for ways to increase the pressure on the target. You may not be able to find any, but the possibility should always be considered.

Now try your hand at the following tests, which focus on relative pins.

Tests

TEST 27. It's White's turn to play. Is Black's position as safe as it seems? Notice that Black's Queen on d7 is undefended. How can White take advantage of this?

TEST 28. Is there any way White can win a pawn from this position?

Van der Wiel–Seirawan
Graz, 1980

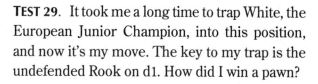

TEST 29. It took me a long time to trap White, the European Junior Champion, into this position, and now it's my move. The key to my trap is the undefended Rook on d1. How did I win a pawn?

TEST 30. It's White's move. Black's Bishop is pinned because any movement it makes will cost the f7-pawn. Unfortunately, White doesn't seem to be able to take advantage of this fact. Can White create any other pins?

TEST 31. Again, it's White's move. Does your solution for the previous test also work here?

TEST 32. Can White win material by pinning?

TEST 33. This test is based on a game between two titans of chess. At the time, Alexander Alekhine was World Champion, and Aaron Nimzovich was itching for a shot at the title. White has tied up his opponent by using a striking series of relative pins on both the c-file and the a4–e8 diagonal. Black is suffering but is managing to hold on. Now it's White's move. How did White put him out of his misery?

Alekhine–Nimzovich
San Remo, 1930

CHAPTER FOUR

The Skewer

A skewer has been likened to a pin in reverse. With a pin, the attacker's objective is to win the pinned piece or the more valuable piece behind it. With a skewer, the attacker's objective is to threaten a valuable piece so that it is forced to move, allowing the capture of a piece behind it.

The position in Diagram 39 illustrates two skewers. White's Bishop on d5 is skewering Black's Rook and Knight, while White's Rook is skewering Black's King and Rook. (If we were to invert Black's two Queen-side pieces and place his Knight on c6 and his Rook on b7, we would have a pin instead of a skewer.) Although Black is a Rook ahead in the starting position, he will finish up on the short end of the material count. First, his

priceless King is in check and is forced to move with **1...Kg6**. White responds with **2.Rxf8**, capturing the skewered Rook. But Black's problems aren't over. He is destined to lose even more material because of the other skewer by the Bishop. After Black moves the Rook on c6, his Knight is lost.

Now let's cement our understanding of the skewer with a few more examples.

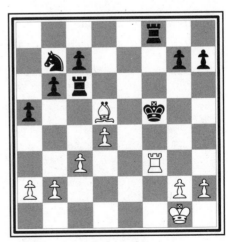

DIAGRAM 39. Black to play.

DIAGRAM 40. White to play.

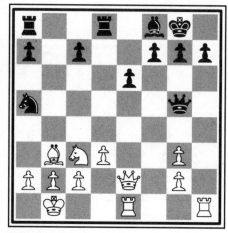

DIAGRAM 41. White to play.

In Diagram 40, White is down an Exchange, but he can still skewer Black's King and Rook and win material with **1.Qh3+**. Now both 1...Qf5 and 1...Qe6 would mean the loss of Black's Queen. Playing 1...Kd8 is impossible because White's Bishop on h4 covers the d8-square, so Black has nothing better than **1...Kc6** or **1...Ke8**, after which **2.Qxc8** grabs the Rook for free.

Now take a look at Diagram 41, where Black has just played the poor

DIAGRAM 42. White to play.

1...Na5??, hoping to chop off White's Bishop on b3. He didn't notice the possibility of **2.Rh5!**, with which White skewers Black's Queen and Knight. After Black orders his Queen's retreat, the Knight on a5 falls, and Black is down a solid 3 points.

In Diagram 42, White's pieces are more active than Black's, and both Black's Bishops are poorly defended. Creating a skewer with **1.Qe4!** is easy. The Bishop on e6 is attacked and if it moves, the poor thing on e7 becomes the sacrifice.

Now let's try some tests. In the following section, you should look for skewers, but if you find something better, don't hesitate to use it!

Tests

TEST 34. What is White's best move?

TEST 35. White is down an Exchange. Find two ways that he can win back the Exchange.

TEST 36. List all of White's possible skewers and then decide which one is best.

CHAPTER FIVE

King Tactics and Combinations

I f you've been attentive, you'll have noticed by now that many tactics are made possible by a weakened or open King. You can ignore an attack on a Knight or Bishop; you can toss your Rooks to the winds; you can sacrifice your Queen; but your King is indispensable. Lose it and the game is over. Because of the finality associated with the King's demise, it stands to reason that several tactics and combinations revolve around this important piece. In this chapter, we will look at tactics and combinations based on stalemate, perpetual check, the destruction of the King's cover, and back rank checkmate.

Stalemate

At times, you will feel that your opponent is picking you apart. First he devours all your pawns; then he dines on a minor piece or two; and finally he carves up your Rooks and Queen. You're left with almost nothing at all... a few survivors and a prayer. At this point in the game, a *stalemate* can become very useful.

A stalemate occurs when it's your turn to move but you don't have a legal move to play. When this happens, the material count becomes meaningless, and the game is declared a draw. In tournament chess, a win is worth 1 point, a draw is worth half a point, and a loss is worth a rather round zero. When your back is against the wall, you will want to try to trick your opponent into capturing more than he should so that you can force a stalemate that will allow you to salvage a critical half-point.

DIAGRAM 43. Black to play.   **DIAGRAM 44. Black to play.**

Diagram 43 is a picture-perfect example of a stalemate. White is 9 points ahead (a full Queen up), but we can see that even such a huge advantage in material does not guarantee a win. The game is a draw because Black is unable to move. His pawns are stuck where they stand, and the b8 and d8 squares are not available because of the presence of the White Queen. This type of draw commonly happens when unwary players think the game is as good as won and stop paying attention!

In Diagram 44, things don't look good for Black. Aside from White's advantage of a Queen vs. a Rook (a 4-point difference), White also threatens multiple checkmates (1.Qc7 Checkmate, 1.Qd7 Checkmate, and 1.Qf8 Checkmate). But closer scrutiny reveals that Black has a chance to save this game. At the moment, his King has no legal moves. Only his Rook can move. All Black has to do is get rid of this Rook, and a stalemate will result. With this idea in mind, you should have no difficulty in spotting Black's best move: **1...Rb6+!**. White has no choice but to take the Rook with **2.Kxb6**. If he doesn't, Black will capture the White Queen after the White King moves out of the way. Unfortunately for White, capturing the Rook gets him nowhere, because Black then finds himself without a move. The loyal Black Rook has sacrificed itself to save its ruler!

DIAGRAM 45. Black to play.   DIAGRAM 46. Black to play.

White, with a two-pawn advantage, is on a roll in Diagram 45. He threatens to pick up the Black Rook with 2.g7+ (a pawn fork). For Black, running away with the Rook by playing 1...Rf1 loses to 2.Re8+ Kg7 3.Rg8 Checkmate or 3.h8=Q Checkmate, and staying on the back rank with 1...Ra8 loses to 2.Kh6 and a quick checkmate. So Black is on the lookout for a stalemate, and he knows that he must somehow get rid of his mobile Rook. Black plays **1...Rf5+!** to which White responds **2.Kg4** (2.Kxf5 produces stalemate, and 2.Kh6 Rh5+! forces White to chop off the Rook). Play continues with **2...Rf4+! 3.Kg3 Rf3+!**. Black keeps checking on the f-file until White tires of the chase, captures the Rook, and allows the stalemate.

Here's another example. In Diagram 46, Black is down two pieces. Normally, he would be tempted to resign the game. Once again though, we have the potential of a stalemated Black King. Because the Queen is the only remaining active member in his army, Black hastens to rid himself of her: **1...Qh2+!! 2.Kxh2** and lo and behold, draw by stalemate! So we have a moral here:

If you are in real trouble but notice that your King has no moves, cheer up and look for a stalemate!

This moral has a flip side:

If you are mashing your opponent and expect him to resign at any moment, don't fall asleep! Be vigilant, or you might be surprised by a game-saving stalemate.

We have been looking at the use of a stalemated King as a last-ditch, loss-avoidance device. Be careful, though, that you don't blunder into a situation where your King is stalemated but the rest of your army has plenty of moves. Imagine that, with a flourish, you sacrifice your army and confidently claim stalemate, only to have your opponent point out that a little pawn at the edge of the board still has a legal move. How embarrassing!

Let's look at a few examples of undesirable stalemates. In Diagram 47, Black's problem lies with his King; it is stalemated and unable to go anywhere. All White has to do is find a check, and the game will end quickly. Because the h7-pawn is pinned by the Rook on h1, **1.Ng6** Checkmate fits the bill rather well.

One of the nicest ways to punish a stalemated King is by way of a *smothered checkmate.* A smothered checkmate occurs when a player's King is boxed in by his own pieces—literally smothered with affection and no place to go. Such a situation is illustrated in Diagram 48. White plays

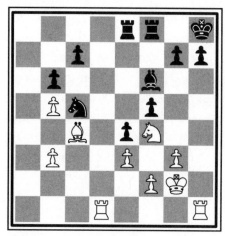

DIAGRAM 47. White to play.

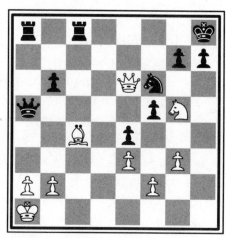

DIAGRAM 48. White to play.

1.Qg8+!!, and after **1...Nxg8** or **1...Rxg8** (1...Kxg8 is impossible because of the Bishop on c4), **2.Nf7** is checkmate.

My favorite smothered checkmate pattern is shown in Diagram 49. Here we have the same position as in Diagram 48, except that White is without his Bishop on c4. Now the "brilliant" 1.Qg8+ would be refuted with the simple 1...Kxg8. However, White can still checkmate with **1.Nf7+ Kg8 2.Nh6++** (a double

DIAGRAM 49. White to play.

check) **2...Kh8** (2...Kf8 allows 3.Qf7 Checkmate) **3.Qg8+!! Rxg8 4.Nf7** Checkmate.

This last example calls to mind a fond memory. When my first chess teacher, Jeffrey Parsons, showed me this smothered checkmate, I was in breathless awe. I ran home to demonstrate it to my mother, who was busy preparing the evening meal. I dragged her over to the chess table and unveiled my newly discovered beauty. "Yasser, that's marvelous!" she said. "Now can I finish cooking?" I realized for the first time that the whole world wasn't enthralled by chess. Boy, just look what they're missing!

Tests

TEST 37. It's Black's turn to play. How can he save himself?

TEST 38. With a two-pawn deficit, White can only hope for a miracle. It's his move. Black's a-pawn is running for a Queen with 1...a3, 2...a2, and 3...a1, and White can do very little to prevent it. Should White give up? Can you see an alternative?

TEST 39. With his extra Rook, Black is winning easily. He would like to checkmate White quickly with 1...Rh6+, but he sees that 2.Qxh6 would thwart this plan. Because White's King has the h4-square and isn't stalemated, Black plays **1...Rg5**, with the powerful threat of 2...Rh5 Checkmate. Is this a wise move for Black?

Bernstein–Smyslov
Groningen, 1946

TEST 40. Black has two extra pawns and is looking for a quick win. Former World Champion Vasily Smyslov decides to finish off his opponent with **1...b2**, because 2.Rxb2 Rh2+ will then skewer the White Rook. Is this a good move?

TEST 41. Black's King is surrounded by White pieces and will soon be checkmated. In desperation, Black plays **1...Qh1+**. Should White now take the Black Queen?

TEST 42. This is one of the greatest saves in chess history. Aside from being up a piece, Black is about to checkmate the White King with ...Re2+. (For example, 1.gxf4 would lose to 1...Re2+ 2.Kh1 Qg2 Checkmate.) Instead of giving up, White sets a devious trap with **1.h4! Re2+ 2.Kh1**. Should Black play 2...Qxg3?

Evans–Reshevsky
New York, 1963

TEST 43. White sees that Black's King has nowhere to run to, and he would love to execute the monarch with a winning check. How can White finish off Black?

Perpetual Check

Another way for a losing player to save an otherwise hopeless position is to engineer a *perpetual check*. This situation comes about when one player repeatedly places his enemy's King in check. The King is harassed back and forth and is unable to escape the series of checks. When a sequence of

DIAGRAM 50. White to play.   DIAGRAM 51. White to play.

moves results in the pieces moving back and forth on the *same squares* and in the *exact same positions* three times, the game is called a *three time repetition of position* and is declared a draw.

Diagram 50 shows a simple case of a perpetual check. Black threatens to checkmate White with 1...Rb8+ or 1...Rf1+, so White must scramble to save himself. Fortunately, an easy draw is available with **1.Qg6+ Kh8 2.Qh6+ Kg8 3.Qg6+**, when the original position is repeated. After three repetitions, either player can claim a draw.

Diagram 51 is another common example of a perpetual check. Black is about to execute the enemy King, but White is able to survive by repeatedly checking Black's monarch. By keeping Black busy with checks, White prevents his opponent from lowering the axe elsewhere on the board. A draw by perpetual check results after **1.Rg7+ Kh8 2.Rh7+ Kg8 3.Rhg7+!**. (This check is with the correct Rook. A terrible mistake would be 3.Rdg7+??, because Black could then cross the d-file with 3...Kf8 4.Rf7+ Ke8 5.Re7+ Kd8 6.Rd7+ Kc8, and then 7.Rc7+ would be met with 7...Qxc7, the winning move for Black.) The game continues with **3...Kf8 4.Rgf7+ Ke8 5.Rfe7+**, and because Black can't cross the barrier on the d-file, he must return to the Kingside and allow the perpetual attack on his King.

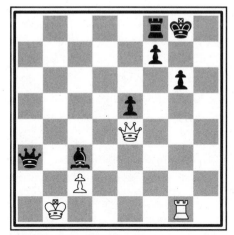

DIAGRAM 52. White to play.

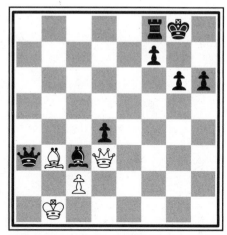

DIAGRAM 53. White to play.

As I've said, you use a perpetual check to save an otherwise inferior or lost game, the goal being not a checkmate but a draw by repetition. But if your opponent refuses to allow the repetition and walks into a checkmate, by all means oblige him!

Let's give the perpetual-check tactic a combinative flair by introducing a sacrifice. In Diagram 52, White is about to be done in with 1...Rb8+, 1...Qb2+, or 1...Qa1+. He must get to the Black King or give up the game. Because the enemy monarch is surrounded by a wall of pawns, White has to crash through this wall and get something going quickly. The slightest hesitation and the game will be over. White snaps into action with **1.Rxg6+!** (uncovering the Black King), and Black is forced to play **1...fxg6.** (Both King moves lose: 1...Kh8?? 2.Qh4 Checkmate and 1...Kh7?? 2.Rg1—discovered check—2...f5 3.Qh4 Checkmate.) The game continues with **2.Qxg6+ Kh8 3.Qh6+** leading to a perpetual check and a subsequent draw.

I have attempted to weave the various tactical themes together in this book so that as we move from one tactic to another, you'll be able to recognize the presence of those I've previously presented. My objective is to make you aware of common patterns so that you can develop your eye for combinations as quickly as possible. In the position in Diagram 53,

DIAGRAM 54. White to play.

1.Qxg6+ is made possible by the absolute pin that White's Bishop has created along the a2–g8 diagonal. After **1...Kh8 2.Qxh6+ Kg8 3.Qg6+**, we have the same perpetual check as in the two previous examples.

Diagram 54 shows another typical perpetual-check pattern. White forces a draw by moving his Queen along the e8–h5 diagonal: **1.Qe8+ Kh7 2.Qh5+ Kg8 3.Qe8+** Draw.

Tests

TEST 44. It's White's move, and he is down a Rook. Is it time to give up? Or can he hang on?

TEST 45. It's White's turn to play. Find the perpetual check.

TEST 46. Black doesn't like the way this game is going because he has less space than his opponent. Looking for a way to bail out, what surprise does he unleash on his opponent?

Grigorian–Jurtaev
USSR, 1979

TEST 47. Black's Rook on a2 is being attacked by White's Queen, but Black is also concerned about White's threat of 1.Re8+ Kh7 2.Qg8+ Checkmate. Does he have any way out of this mess?

Domuls–Staerman
USSR, 1978

Destroying the King's Cover

All chess players love to hunt down the enemy King. But capturing the King isn't easy. Usually the King sprints by castling to the Kingside, where he is protected behind the pawns on f2, g2, and h2. To get at such an entrenched monarch, a player will often sacrifice a piece or two to draw the supposedly safe King out into hostile territory. When the King is floating around in the center without cover, he usually perishes because the enemy pieces can quickly hunt him down. If you sense such a checkmating possibility, throw aside any material concerns. Even if you are many pieces down, a checkmate always ends the struggle in your favor.

DIAGRAM 55. White to play.

DIAGRAM 56. White to play.

Diagram 55 shows a classic checkmating pattern. By covering both files, White is able to play **1.Rh1** Checkmate. Let's carry this idea into a more complicated setting. In Diagram 56, both players are trying to get at each other's King. Black threatens White's King with 1...Qb2 Checkmate. Black's King is weakened by the absence of the g7-pawn but seems safely tucked behind the h7-pawn. Because this pawn is all that protects the Black King, White must find a method of blowing the pawn away and creating the checkmating position shown in Diagram 55. Playing without kid gloves, White kicks the pawn off the board with **1.Qxh7+!**. Without pawns surrounding it, Black's King is fair game for White's Rooks, and **1...Kxh7 2.Rh1** produces checkmate. The fact that White is down a Queen in the final position is meaningless. In fact, a Queen sacrifice that leads to checkmate is most satisfying. Try it yourself sometime.

Diagram 57 is a famous example of a King being forced into hostile territory. It is considered one of the world's most beautiful combinations. Black plays **1...Qxh3+!!**, giving up his Queen but dragging the White King forward into the jaws of doom. Play continues with **2.Kxh3 Rh6+ 3.Kg4**.

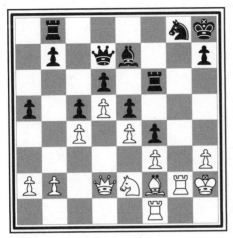

DIAGRAM 57. White to play.
Averbakh–Kotov
Zürich, 1953

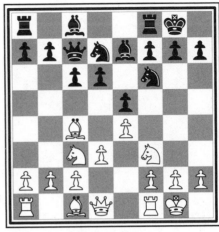

DIAGRAM 58. White to play.

(Running up the board with his King isn't what White wants to do, but he has no choice.) Now **3...Nf6+ 4.Kf5** leads to the paradoxical **4...Ng4!!**. Black blocks the White Rook from participating in the defense and threatens the killing ...Rf8+. Both **5.fxg4 Rf8+** and **5.Kxg4 Rg8+ 6.Kf5 Rf6** lead to checkmate. This example shows how formidable Rooks are as hunters when a King is opened up.

A common mistake made by beginners is thinking that the enemy King is in trouble when it has been drawn only to the second rank. Sometimes, the King is indeed in trouble, but usually it can simply step back into its original position. Faced with the position in Diagram 58, many a White player has tried **1.Ng5 h6 2.Nxf7?! Rxf7 3.Bxf7+ Kxf7**. This isn't a good maneuver for White. Black's King can easily step back to safety with 4...Kg8, and though the material count is even (6 points vs. 6 points), two pieces are usually considered superior to a Rook and a pawn in the middlegame, because two pieces represent two strong attacking units vs. the Rook's one. (The extra pawn is only useful in an endgame.)

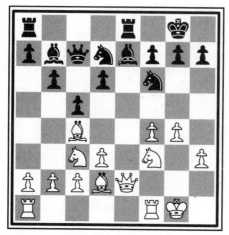

DIAGRAM 59. White to play.

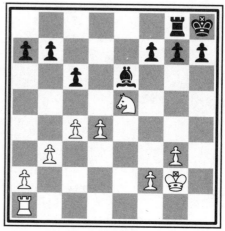

DIAGRAM 60. Black to play.

If you want to be successful with a capture on f7, you must draw the King even further into the center of the board. Diagram 59 offers a lively illustration of how to do this. We have seen how dangerous it is for a King to be drawn out into the open. Here, White finds a novel way of inviting Black's King to come to the party: **1.Bxf7+! Kxf7**. The King has poked his head out the door. However, if he can go back into his hole with ...Kg8, then White's sacrifice will have been in vain. It's time to grab him and pull him into the open. White plays **2.Qe6+!!**, offering up his Queen as well! Now Black's retreat with 2...Kf8 loses to 3.Ng5, and 4.Qf7 Checkmate is hard to stop. Black decides to take the gift and steps into the middle of the board with **2...Kxe6**. The response: **3.Ng5** Checkmate!

Diagram 60 shows another example. Here, Black's position is perfectly alright, and he should play 1...Rd8, putting pressure on White's d4-pawn. Instead, he thinks it might be nice to get rid of White's Knight, so he decides to chase the Knight away with **1...f6??**. The roof unexpectedly caves in after **2.Ng6+! hxg6 3.Rh1+**, when Black has to play **3...Bh3+** and allow **4.Rxh3** Checkmate.

What happened here? It's very simple. When your King is stalemated or has few moves available, a warning light should start flashing in your head. A King with limited ability to move is very vulnerable, because any check could easily result in checkmate. All the attacker has to do is find a way to break into his majesty's chambers. One of the good points of 1...Rd8 is that it gives the King access to the g8-square, thus ending any worries about the type of massacre we just witnessed. The moral is:

Try to keep the pawn cover in front of your King intact and be sure your King has room to breathe.

Tests

TEST 48. It's White's move. Black's King is nice and snug behind his pawns. What can White do to change things?

TEST 49. Black's Rooks and Queen don't seem to be able to finish off White. Can you find a way for Black to bring in another attacking unit?

TEST 50. White's pieces are clustered around Black's King, but the Black pawns on g7 and h6 are holding the fort. Realizing that he is a pawn down, White has to find some way to break through. Quiet maneuvers won't get the job done. This is a tough one. Can you find a forcing continuation that wins the game for White?

**Hort–Seirawan
Bad Kissingen, 1981**

TEST 51. My opponent in this game, the Czech Grandmaster Vlastimil Hort, has a reputation for tricking his opponents with tactical play. I have deliberately captured his b2-pawn, and Hort has played a Knight fork, winning a Rook. At this point, I find a complicated way of destroying the White King's pawn cover with one of my best combinations. What did I do? It's alright if you don't see this one through to the end. What's important is that you learn to recognize the value of making an enemy King vulnerable to direct attack. If you can get the first four moves, give yourself a pat on the back.

**Edward Lasker–
Sir George Thomas
London, 1911**

TEST 52. A wonderful classic from the treasure chest of combinations. White sees that uncovering the Bishop's attack on the h7-square with 1.Nxf6+ fails when Black's Queen defends with 1...gxf6. What beautiful scheme did White come up with to create a King hunt?

Back Rank Checkmate

A back rank checkmate occurs when the King is on the back rank; its pawn shield is in place, preventing it from moving up the board; and it is under attack by the enemy Queen or Rook. When the King has nowhere to run, the check is deadly. The pattern that produces back rank checkmate is one of the most common and most important in chess. Every player at one point or another has fallen victim to a back rank checkmate. The mere threat of

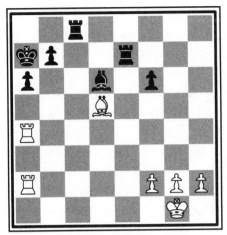

DIAGRAM 61. White to play.

DIAGRAM 62. White to play.

it strikes fear into the hearts of experienced players. As a result, moves such as h3 and ...h6 or g3 and ...g6 are quite common. In chess terms, moves like these are called *making luft*. (*Luft* is a German word meaning *air*.) Giving the King "air" (room to breathe; in other words, an escape square) eliminates the back rank problem once and for all.

Our first example (Diagram 61) shows how to avoid a back rank checkmate by making *luft*. Black threatens to checkmate White on the back rank with 1...Rc1 Checkmate or 1...Re1 Checkmate. How can White prevent his King's demise? If he plays 1.Ra1, his Rook will be stuck on the back rank, playing nursemaid to the King. The usual method of dealing with Black's back rank checkmate threat is for White to move one of the pawns that imprison his King, playing either 1.h3 or 1.g3. However, before deciding on this course of action, White must consider what the other Black pieces are doing. Here, 1.h3 still allows 1...Rc1 Checkmate, because Black's Bishop is controlling the h2-square. The correct move is **1.g3**, which limits the scope of Black's Bishop and gives the King the comfortable g2-square to run to.

The simple goal of trapping a cornered King on the back rank is the driving force behind many combinations. Diagram 62 illustrates a common back rank checkmating sequence. Black seems to be defending his back

DIAGRAM 63. White to play.

rank with his Rook, but after sacrificing the White Queen with **1.Qe8+!**, White forces checkmate with **1...Rxe8 2.Rxe8** Checkmate.

In Diagram 63, Black's King is tucked away in a corner, and the back rank is weak. Moreover, Black is woefully behind in development because his Bishop has nowhere safe to go. As good as things look for White, he is unable to finish off his opponent because Black's Queen is keeping White's Rook from playing Re8. White's goal is clear: Make the e8-square available for the Rook, and checkmate will follow. In light of this goal, the suicidal **1.Qd6!** makes a lot of sense. White offers up his Queen, knowing that if she is taken, the e8-square will no longer be defended. Because 1...Qg8 and 1...Qf7 fail to 2.BxQ and 1...Qxd6 2.Re8+ leads to checkmate, Black has no choice: He must throw away his Bishop with 1...Bd7 or 1...Be6 to keep his back rank safely protected. However, after **1...Bd7 2.Qxd7**, the loss of the Bishop still leads eventually to a White victory.

We have seen that a weak back rank is a serious problem—one to be carefully avoided in your games. Inexperienced players are often so caught up in their plans that they don't take the time to ensure their King's safety. A good rule of thumb is to make some *luft* as soon as you see future back rank problems looming. Be especially careful when the center of the board starts to clear and the enemy Rooks have open files. On the other hand, if your opponent seems to be neglecting his back rank, start looking for possibilities that might lead to a back rank checkmate.

I've made a couple of changes to the previous position to produce Diagram 64. One big difference is that White's back rank is now weak, but Black doesn't seem to be in any position to take advantage of it. If White thinks he can win with the same moves as in the previous example, then

DIAGRAM 64. White to play.

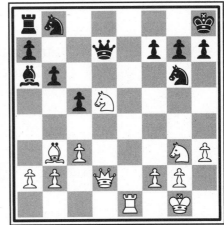

DIAGRAM 65. White to play.

he's in for a surprise. Play proceeds: **1.Qd6 Bd7! 2.Qxd7??**. White snaps up the Bishop because he thinks the extra piece will lead to an easy win. To his surprise, he loses his Queen when Black plays **2...Rd8!**. Suddenly the roles are reversed! Black is pinning the White Queen to the opposite back rank, and Queen moves, such as 3.Qxb7, allow 3...Rd1+ followed by checkmate.

If, after **1.Qd6 Bd7!**, White notices the rude trap that Black has set, he might try **2.Qxf8+ Rxf8 3.Re7** in the hopes of getting a good endgame. However, Black can still use a pin and take advantage of White's weak back rank to make life easier for himself with **3...Re8!**. Then **4.Rxd7?? Re1** is checkmate. Alternatively, 4.Rxe8+ Bxe8 should lead to a draw.

By now, you probably have a sense of how tactics can be combined to take advantage of a weak back rank. In the previous example, we saw the effectiveness of a pin combined with a back rank checkmate. Diagram 65 shows how a back rank problem can also make forks and double attacks stronger than usual. Black's Queen is stuck guarding the e8-square, and the normally impossible **1.Nc7!** is now an excellent move because of possibilities like 1...Qxc7 (or 1...Qxd2) 2.Re8+ Nf8 3.Rxf8 Checkmate. Faced with threats of 2.Re8+ and 2.Nxa8, Black resigns the game.

Tests

TEST 53. It's Black's move. Seeing that White's Rook cannot penetrate his position because the e8-square is defended three times, Black is tempted to play 1...Rxa2 and grab a material advantage. Should Black take this pawn?

TEST 54. Is the greedy 1...Qxa2 a worthwhile move for Black?

TEST 55. Is 1.Qe8+ a winner for White from this position?

TEST 56. To Black, grabbing the a2-pawn with 1...Qxa2 seems a fine move. Can you see why this move would lose him the game?

CHAPTER SIX

Deflection

At times, you might find yourself on the brink of victory, except that your opponent clings to life as hard as he can. As often as not, his tough defense is made possible by one hard-working piece that is somehow holding everything together. To break down such a position, you need to chase the defender away from the critical area in the hopes that the defense will then fall apart. Preventing the main defending piece from performing its duties usually reduces the opponent's army to chaos. This concept is the basis of the tactic known as *deflection*.

The concept of the *overworked piece* is, to my mind, virtually the same as the concept of deflection. An overworked piece is one that is asked to do too much: The piece performs double duty, if you will. All you need to do is pull it aside, at which point its duties will be left undone.

Here's an example. In Diagram 66, Black is behind a pawn and, understandably, wants to get back his lost material. He plays **1...Qxb2??** and feels pretty satisfied. After all, his Queen is well defended by his Bishop. Unfortunately, Black has placed this Bishop in an overworked position. The Bishop not only has to defend the Queen, but must also block any checks that materialize on the back rank. This double duty leads to immediate disaster after **2.Rd8+,**

DIAGRAM 66. **Black to play.**

because Black has no choice but to play **2...Bf8**. Then after **3.Qxb2**, his poor Queen is whisked off the board.

Until now, I've focused on the thought processes of the attacker. Let's switch for a moment to the point of view of the defender—not as much fun, but we'll get back to the attack soon enough. For now, let's defend.

We've seen that undefended pieces make ripe tactical targets, so you know that defending your pieces is important. The best defenders are pawns. They are slow and small, but they make excellent supporters. However, be careful when your pieces have to defend one another; the results can be disastrous. Often, a defending piece can simply be chased away, as Diagram 67 illustrates. Here, material is even, but Black's Knight on b3 is hanging. Black's best move is the retreat 1...Nbc5, which allows White to devour an extra pawn with 2.Rxb6. Not thrilled with such a possibility, Black defends the b3-Knight with **1...Nec5??**. In his efforts to save a pawn, Black ends up losing a piece. White's **2.d4** puts the c5-Knight under attack, and if that Knight moves, the one on b3 falls.

In Diagram 68, White has just played Qd3, offering to trade Queens. Black is not averse to this arrangement, but he wants to trade on his own terms. So, instead of the safe 1...Qxd3, Black plays **1...Rd8??**. This move also appears safe, until you consider that this Rook is the Queen's only

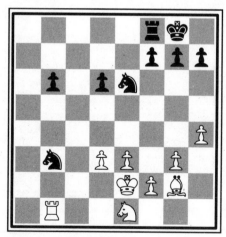

DIAGRAM 67. Black to play.

DIAGRAM 68. Black to play.

74

bodyguard. Small wonder, then, that **2.Re8+!** leads to a forced win of material. If Black plays 2...Rxe8, the Queen's sole defender is deflected, and the simple 3.Qxd5 does the job. The other possiblity, 2...Kg7, allows 3.Rxd8, after which White has devoured a Rook for a 5-point gain. This method of drawing off a defender is commonly used and must be carefully guarded against.

Black threatens to win with

DIAGRAM 69. Black to play.

...Qxf2+ in Diagram 69, but at the moment he is in check and must decide how best to get out of it. The correct defense is 1...Kf8, after which 2.Rxh7 or 2.Qxh7 loses to the threatened ...Qxf2+. Instead, Black plays it "safe" with **1...Qf7??** and loses the house after **2.Rxh7+!**, when his King is forced to abandon the defense of his lady. The game continues with **2...Kxh7 3.Qxf7+**, and then—horror of horrors—Black loses everything because his King and Rook are forked!

In all of these examples, the defender's mistake was relying on his *pieces* to defend one another. Of course, pieces are capable of defense, but sometimes you have to be careful that your defending piece doesn't become the victim of a deflection tactic.

So far, we've looked at simple cases of deflection and overworked pieces. But this tactic can occasionally produce very involved, exquisite combinations. The position in Diagram 70 on the next page is one of the most beautiful examples of an overworked piece and the art of deflection. It is a classic.

Black's Rook on e8 is under pressure from White's Rooks, but Black's Queen seems to be holding everything together. Noticing that Black is

75

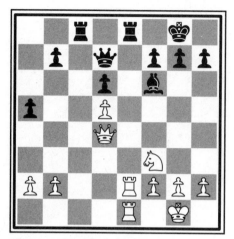

DIAGRAM 70. **Black to play.**
Adams–Torre
New Orleans, 1920

suffering from a potential back rank weakness, White then decides to do everything possible to deflect the Black Queen from the defense of the e8-Rook. He attacks the Queen with **1.Qg4!**, forcing her to flee. Because 1...Qxg4 2.Rxe8+ Rxe8 3.Rx8 produces checkmate, Black plays **1...Qb5**, which leads to **2.Qc4!!**. Once again, White's Queen attacks her Black counterpart, but this time two Black pieces can capture the impudent White Queen. Black chooses **2...Qd7** because both 2...Rxc4 and 2...Qxc4 lead to checkmate after 3.Rxe8+. White seems to have gone crazy when he plays **3.Qc7!!**, but he's still trying to pull Black's pieces away from the defense of the e8-Rook. If either Black piece takes White's Queen, then a checkmate on e8 will occur. Play continues with **3...Qb5 4.a4!** (more harassment of the poor Black Queen) **4...Qxa4 5.Re4!** (threatening 6.Qxc8!, when 6...Rxc8 7.Rxa4 leaves White with an extra Rook) **5...Qb5** (5...Rxc7 is still impossible due to 6.Rxe8 Checkmate) **6.Qxb7!**. Now Black's Queen has nowhere to run to! Because 6...Qxb7 7.Rxe8+ leads to checkmate, Black resigns the game.

This complicated battle deserves close scrutiny, and I recommend that you play it over several times until you thoroughly understand the ideas and variations.

Now for some tests. To solve the problems in this section, take a long, hard look at enemy pieces that are attacked or overworked, and then find a way to make these factors work for you.

76

Tests

TEST 57. It's White's move. The only defender of the Black Knight is the Bishop on d6. How can White take advantage of this position?

TEST 58. If White's Rook were not on the h-file, Black could win the game with 1...Rh2+ 2.Kg1 Reg2 Checkmate. How can Black make this fantasy variation a reality?

Hjorth–Lundin
Motala, 1946

TEST 59. I played into this position to set up my opponent for a deflection tactic. Only one piece is guarding the Knight on c8 and the Bishop on f6. How did I exploit this fact?

Seirawan–Sulsky
Vancouver, 1981

Seirawan–Henley
Memphis, 1976

TEST 60. This position is taken from my first US Junior Championship. My opponent has sacrificed a piece for a few pawns. His back rank is not defended, and if I can lure his Queen away from the protection of e8, then Qe8 would be checkmate. How did I accomplish this goal?

TEST 61. White is down the Exchange, but he has a strong attack and it's his turn to play. Notice that any move by the Rook on g8 would allow Qg7 Checkmate, while Black's Queen must protect his f7-pawn or face Nxf7 Checkmate. How can White lure Black's pieces away from their important defensive posts?

CHAPTER SEVEN

Battery on an Open File or Diagonal

A s you gain experience, you'll learn that open files and diagonals are crucial for Rooks and Bishops if you want them to play an active part in the game. Many players don't realize the advantages of reinforcing control of files and diagonals by *doubling* the pieces on these open lines. By putting two Rooks on a file or a Queen and a Bishop on a diagonal, you can create situations where the lead piece can make excursions into enemy territory under the watchful protection of its backup piece. (Because the Queen and the Rooks move in similar ways, it's sometimes even possible to *triple* on a file, though not on a diagonal.) Doubling on a file or diagonal is known as *creating a battery*. Batteries are the powerhouse punches of chess, and any opportunity to create one must be carefully cultivated.

Playing Down an Open File

When both players have pawns on the same file, the file is closed. When no pawns are on a file, the file is open. And when only one player's pawn is on a file, the file is half-open. Open files are the Rook's highways into the opponent's position. In particular, the 7th rank is usually the Rook's strongest position and is sometimes referred to as the "refreshment rank." A Rook on the 7th rank refreshes itself by munching on enemy pawns while simultaneously eyeing the enemy King. Many authorities go so far as to say that getting a Rook on the 7th rank is worth a pawn sacrifice. Let's look at some examples.

DIAGRAM 71. White to play.

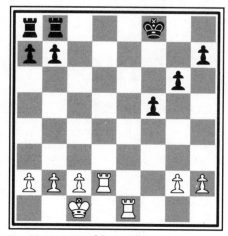

DIAGRAM 72. White to play.

By playing **1.Rd7** in Diagram 71, White forks the h-pawn and b-pawn. He also ties down Black's King on the 8th rank. The difference between the potential activity of the two Rooks is now striking. Always do your best to ensure the activity of your Rooks. Too often, players try to develop their Bishops, Knights, and Queen but do little to bring their Rooks into the battle.

As strong as a Rook on the 7th rank is, doubled Rooks on the 7th are even stronger. Often called *pigs on the 7th*, doubled rooks on the 7th rank attack the enemy pieces with the ferocity of wild boars. Such colorful expressions, whatever their origins, certainly help impress upon us how powerful these Rooks become. In Diagram 72, White plays **1.Rd7**, and if Black defends his h-pawn with **1...Kg8**, then **2.Ree7** obliterates him. Here's an example: **2...h5 3.Rg7+ Kf8 4.Rxg6**. Black loses several pawns.

Placing two Rooks on the 7th produces such a strong position that sacrificing a pawn to achieve it is a real bargain. From the position shown in Diagram 73, White plays **1.Re7!**, to which Black responds **Rxf5**. (If Black defends with 1...Rf7, then 2.Rxf7 Kxf7 3.Rd7+ gives White an active Rook and Black a passive one, leaving Black badly tied up.) Now **2.Rdd7** means Black will lose his Kingside pawns as well as some of his Queen-side pawns.

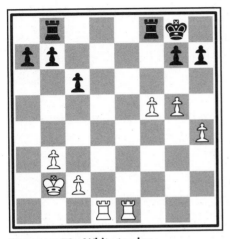

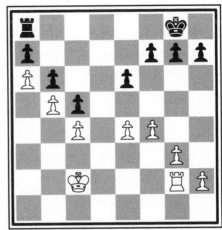

DIAGRAM 73. White to play.

DIAGRAM 74. White to play.

Understanding the importance of the 7th rank makes it easier to appreciate the usefulness of an open file. In Diagram 74, Black would be in good shape if he could take the d-file with 1...Rd8 or if he could prevent White from penetrating it with 1...Kf8 followed by 2...Ke7. But unfortunately for Black, it is White's move. By playing **1.Rd2**, White lays claim to the d-file, and Black is powerless to prevent the charge to the 7th.

The position in Diagram 75 is almost identical to that in Diagram 74. The difference is that each side has a second Rook. Now when White goes after the d-file with **1.Rd2**, Black is able to mount a challenge with **1...Rfd8**. However, White's ability to double his Rooks and create a battery enables him to dominate the d-file with **2.Rad1! Rxd2+ 3.Rxd2**. Once again, Black is unable to stop White's inevitable jump to the 7th.

The domination of files by doubling Rooks on them is considered a

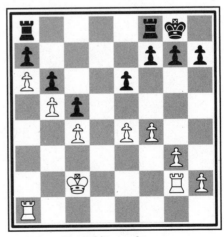

DIAGRAM 75. White to play.

strategy rather than a tactic. A Russian children's rhyme goes:

It's very practical but just not tactical!

However, when you add such batteries to tactics like pins, double attacks, and back rank checkmates, you open up a whole world of combinative possibilities!

Diagram 76 shows an example of doubling and tripling on a file combined with themes of double attack and use of the pin. When White plays **1.Bxh7!**, Black can try the following defenses:

- ■ **1...Kxh7**, which leads to **2.Qd3+** (a double attack against h7 and d7) **2...Kg8 3.Rxd7**. White has won a pawn.

- ■ **1...g6**, which traps the Bishop (Black hopes to win it later). White then plays **2.Qd2**, creating a triple battery on the pinned Knight and ensuring that after Black picks up the trapped Bishop, White will enjoy a one-pawn advantage.

- ■ **1...e5** or **1...c5**, both of which are met with **2.Rd6** and variations similar to those produced by the previous two defenses.

An open file is particularly useful if it provides a route to the enemy King's encampment and can be used for a checkmating raid. In Diagram 77, White threatens to end the game with Qh8 or Qh7 Checkmate, knowing

DIAGRAM 76. White to play.

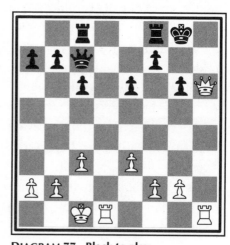

DIAGRAM 77. Black to play.

that his Queen is firmly backed up by the Rook on h1. Black's only defense is **1...f6**, after which **2.Qh8+** (2.Qxg6+ Qg7 3.Qxg7+ Kxg7 4.Rd7+ Rf7 5.Rxf7+ Kxf7 6.Rh7+ followed by 7.Rxb7 is also adequate for a win) **2...Kf7 3.Rh7+ Ke8 4.Rxc7 Rxh8 5.Rxc8+** skewers Black's other Rook.

In Diagram 78, the h-file is only half open because Black has a pawn on h7. White would like to use the half-open h-file to play for check-

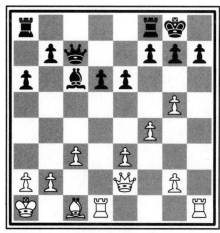

DIAGRAM 78. White to play.

mate. He is willing to give up a lot of material to reach his goal, but a direct move like 1.Qh5 (threatening 2.Qxh7 Checkmate) allows 1...Be4 (defending the h7-pawn), whereas 1.Qd3 f5 2.gxf6 e.p. (*en passant*) gxf6 brings Black's Queen to the defense of the h7-pawn. So White plays with the intention of opening the deadly h-file by sacrificing a Rook: **1.Rxh7! Kxh7 2.Qh5+ Kg8 3.Rh1** (creating a battery on the h-file) **3...f6**. Black's third move is the only way to stop 4.Qh8 Checkmate. Black is hoping for 4.Qh8+ Kf7, which will allow him to run with his King. However, White's next move closes the escape hatch: **4.g6!**. Black's entombed King is doomed because 5.Qh8 Checkmate is inevitable and the King has nowhere to run.

Now try your hand at a few tests. Those that follow all involve Rooks on open files combined with tactics.

Tests

TEST 62. This position is an example of a discovered attack made possible by the battery of White's Rooks on the open d-file. It's White's move. How can he best take advantage of the situation?

TEST 63. White controls the game because of his iron grip on the d-file. Black can't move either of his Rooks, or he will lose his Knight to Rxd7. Moreover, his Knight is pinned because moving it results in the loss of the d8-Rook. How can White take advantage of this very favorable situation?

TEST 64. Black is exerting some unpleasant pressure on White's a2-pawn. It's White's turn to play. How can he relieve this pressure?

TEST 65. This test is quite a bit harder than the others, but its difficulty also makes it the prettiest! White has sacrificed a piece and a pawn to be able to mount an attack along the h-file, but Black has managed to block the attack by placing his Knight on h5. Can White break through?

Playing on an Open Diagonal

Open diagonals are to Bishops what open files are to Rooks. If you have Bishops on the board, it's important to place them on long, open diagonals so that they can constantly threaten to swoop down on the enemy position. Significantly, in chaturanga, the ancient Indian precursor of chess, Bishops were the equivalent of archers, who were considered to be good protectors and, given a view, fine attackers. Always be on the alert for ways to open up your position in order to give your Bishops more room to operate. Let's look at a few Bishops and the havoc they can wreak.

In Diagram 79, Black is up two Exchanges and a pawn, and it's his move. Nevertheless, he is dead in the water. Why? Because the Black King is stalemated, so any check is checkmate. In addition, White's two beautiful Bishops are scoping out their long diagonals. Black's troubles are obvious. White threatens to checkmate with **Bb2+**, and Black is powerless to prevent it.

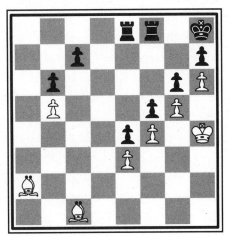

DIAGRAM 79. Black to play.

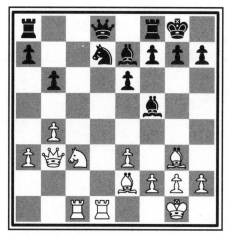

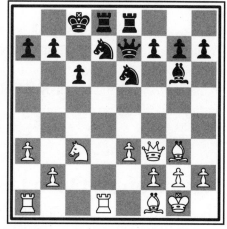

DIAGRAM 80. White to play.　　　DIAGRAM 81. White to play.

The position in Diagram 80 is rather mundane, but it does demonstrate that Bishops are a danger to all enemy pieces if they manage to find good diagonals. Here, White hunts down the poor Black Rook with **1.Bf3 Rc8 2.Bb7**, at which point the Rook has no escape and will soon be captured.

Diagram 81 is a classic case of a King being restricted in its movements by a Bishop. Black's King is stalemated. As I discussed in Chapter Five, White must try to find a way to break through because any lasting check will be the last check! In this case, White makes an elegant Queen sacrifice with **1.Qxc6+!**, which allows the innocent-looking Bishop on f1 to decisively join the game. After **1...bxc6**, **2.Ba6** is checkmate.

As strong as a Bishop dominating a diagonal can be, you can often augment its power by placing the Queen on the same diagonal. Such a battery can be as potent as doubling Rooks on a file.

In Diagram 82, Black's position looks safe enough, but White is able to win a pawn by doubling on the b1–h7 diagonal via **1.Qd3!**. White then threatens 2.Qh7 Checkmate. Black is forced to play **1...g6**, after which **2.Bxh6** picks up the now-undefended h6-pawn.

DIAGRAM 82. White to play.

DIAGRAM 83. White to play.

The position in Diagram 83 allows White to show his power on the a1–h8 diagonal with **1.Qc3**. Black is then powerless to prevent the threats of **2.Qh8** or **2.Qg7** Checkmate. (The f7-pawn can't block with 1...f6 because it is held in an absolute pin by the Bishop at c4.)

Notice how Bishops can be particularly effective when operating on adjacent diagonals. Many of the great combinations of chess history have arisen because Bishops on adjacent diagonals have been trained on the enemy King's position.

Tests

TEST 66. Black has a material advantage of two Knights vs. a Rook, for a 1-point edge. What can White play to show the power of his Bishops?

TEST 67. It's Black's move. White threatens to fork Black's Queen and Rook with Nc5. Is **1...Bxa4** a good defense?

TEST 68. Again, it's Black's move. Is **1...b5**, which attacks White's Bishop on c4, a good idea?

TEST 69. If you learned your lesson from Diagram 81, you will be the master of this situation. It's White's turn to play. No quiet moves here. Can you shatter the Black position?

CHAPTER EIGHT

The Power of Pawns

I
n the middlegame, pawns dominate the center and help control space. As the game progresses and pieces are traded, a change takes place. The pawns, acting like salmon, try hard to swim up the board and realize their potential for promotion. The legendary Grandmaster Aaron Nimzovich called this activity "the pawn's lust to expand." Without a doubt, the "queening of a pawn" is a momentous occasion, and being able to participate in this ritual is worth a great expenditure of time and material. In the following diagrams, the goal is to sacrifice material—the hallmark of a combination—so that a pawn will receive its promotion.

In Diagram 84, White can entertain hopes of winning if he can promote his lone remaining pawn to a Queen. He plays **1.f7**. Black will do anything to stop the promotion, including sacrificing his Bishop, so he responds with **1...Bc5**. Now White can win a piece with 2.Bg7 followed by 3.f8+Q, but after 3...Bxf8, White will be left with only one piece. The result will be a draw because a King and a Bishop cannot checkmate a lone King. So instead of scooping up Black's Bishop, White plays **2.Bd4!**, sacrificing his own Bishop to promote his pawn. This move is an immediate winner because 2...Bxd4 allows 3.f8=Q, and White's King and Queen can easily overcome Black's King and Bishop. Note that Black's Bishop can't escape with 2...Bd6 because of the absolute pin.

DIAGRAM 84. White to play.

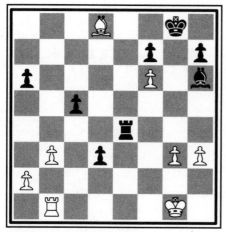

DIAGRAM 85. **Black to play.**
Seredenko–Belousov
USSR, 1972

By now, this concept should be perfectly clear: If the result of the game depends on the queening of a pawn, you must do everything possible—including sacrificing pieces and other pawns—to accomplish this goal.

Diagram 85 offers another example. Here, material is even, but Black's pawn on d3 has more queening potential than any of its brothers. The plan is clear: Turn this pawn into a Queen or force White to give up a decisive amount of material to stop the promotion. Normally a move like 1...d2 is strong. A White response of 2.Kf2? Rd4, with the double threat of 3...Rxd8 and 3...d1=Q, wins Black a piece, whereas 2.Rd1? Re1+ is even worse for White. A stronger defense is 2.Ba5!. Because White's Bishop now helps control the e1-square, 2...Re1+ no longer works, and 3.Rd1 and 4.Kf2 lead to a draw.

To win the position in Diagram 85, Black needs something more extreme: **1...Bc1!!** fits the bill. This fine move blocks White's Rook and threatens 2...d2, 3...d1=Q+, and a win. Because 2.Rxc1 d2 produces the double threat of 3...dxc1=Q and 3...Re1+ (another win), White has to play **2.Ba5**, leading to **2...d2 3.Bxd2 Bxd2**. Down a piece and seeing no prospects, White resigns.

In Diagram 86, White desperately wants to queen his h5-pawn, but a direct run with 1.h6 fails to 1...f4 2.h7 f5, as Black's Bishop covers the queening square. The advance of Black's f-pawns is what enables Black's Bishop to cover the h8 queening square, so White decides to block these pawns with the suicidal **1.Bf4!** Black now gives up because **1...Kxf4 2.h6** leads to the creation of a new White Queen.

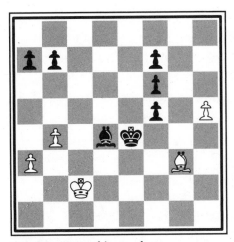

DIAGRAM 86. White to play.
Everz–Kiffmeyer
Germany, 1964

DIAGRAM 87. White to play.

When a pawn is unopposed on a file and no enemy pawn can impede its advancement by capturing it, then the pawn has achieved the exalted status of a *passed pawn*. We have seen how important it is to queen your passed pawns before your opponent can queen his. Often, though, your pawns will not be passed, and you will be forced to find ways to get them by the enemy's sentries.

Diagram 87 is a classic example of how to sneak a pawn through. Both players have exactly the same set of pawns, and it is hard to imagine either side creating a "passer." However, White can force one of his pawns through using a sequence of moves called a *breakthrough combination*. White sacrifices two pawns to get one promoted. Here's how he does it: **1.g6! hxg6** (1...fxg6 2.h6! gxh6 3.f6 queens the f-pawn) **2.f6!**, threatening 3.fxg7. Black is forced to capture with **2...gxf6**. White plays **3.h6**, ensuring that his newly passed pawn will be queened. Although Black now has *connected passed pawns*, they are much slower than White's pawn, which is farther up the board.

The breakthrough combination works only if your pawns are closer to queening than your opponent's. (Note that if it were Black's move in

Diagram 87, he would be able to dash all White's hopes because 1...g6! 2.hxg6 hxg6 creates an impenetrable blockade.) You should commit the position in Diagram 87 to memory because it occurs often in the games of chess masters.

The important breakthrough combination comes in various sacrificial forms. Often a piece will sacrifice itself so that the pawns can get a running start. Let's take a look at a simple illustration. In Diagram 88, White wins by blowing away the Black pawns that are blockading his own pawns with **1.Nxf6! gxf6** (if Black doesn't capture the Knight, White plays 2.Nh5 followed by 3.Nxg7) **2.g7**, leading to the coronation of the g-pawn.

The next example shows the breakthrough combination in a more complicated setting. Diagram 89 is a mixture of the concepts presented in Diagrams 87 and 88. Black's pawn on g3 is the closest one to queening, but at the moment, it is firmly blocked by its White counterpart. By sacrificing a piece, Black sets off a chain reaction: **1...Nxd5+! 2.exd5 e4!** (Black threatens to free the g-pawn with 3...exf3 4.gxf3 g2 and a queening)

DIAGRAM 88. White to play.

DIAGRAM 89. Black to play.
Scholz–Lorens
Correspondence, 1964

3.Nc4 (another hopeless move is 3.fxe4 f3! 4.gxf3 g2, which also gives Black's King a new bride) **3...exf3 4.Nd2 f2!** (a key move; the alternative 4...fxg2?? 5.Nf3 is a bad mistake that leaves Black's pawn firmly blocked by the Knight) **5.Kd3 f3!** (finally, White's important g2-blocker is destroyed) **6.gxf3** (if White plays 6.Nx f3, then f1=Q produces an instant Queen) **6...g2**. At last, Black's pawns have forced their way through. White resigns.

Now let's look at some tests that involve breakthrough combinations. Good luck!

Tests

TEST 70. Black can't win with ...Bb6, ...Bg1, and ...Bxh2. Can you find the move that produces immediate results?

TEST 71. White's two pawns on the 6th rank are nearly home. He would like to play 1.fxe7, but then 1...Rxe6 stops both pawns' progress. Also useless are 1.f7 Rf6 and 1.Rxc5 Rxf6. Can you help White promote a pawn?

Skuratov–Sveshnikov
USSR, 1969

Spassky–Larsen
Palma de Mallorca, 1969

TEST 72. Here, former World Champion Boris Spassky is a pawn down. It's White's turn to play, and he manages to make Black resign in just two moves. Did Spassky win with magic or just fancy play?

Svacina–H. Muller
Vienna, 1941

TEST 73. It's Black's turn to play, and he appears to be in serious trouble. If his King moves, White will take the d5-pawn. Any pawn move also leads to pawn losses. Should Black resign?

Underpromotion

After a long grueling march up the board, the pawn's reward for its efforts is to *choose* which piece other than a King it wants to become. Nine times out of ten, the pawn will want to become a Queen. However, on rare occasions it will opt to change into a less valuable piece. When a pawn chooses to become a piece other than a Queen, it is using a tactic called *underpromotion.* The main reasons for this decision are to avoid stalemate or to try for a Knight fork. Let's start with avoiding stalemate.

In Diagam 90, White would love to make a Queen with 1.c8=Q, but he notices that this move leads to a stalemate. Not wishing to throw away his obviously winning advantage, White instead plays **1.c8=R!**, knowing that **2.Rc7** will lead to a win.

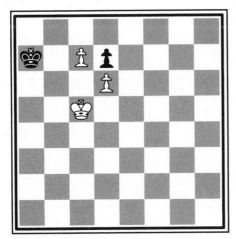

DIAGRAM 90. White to play.

DIAGRAM 91. White to play.

Stalemate possibilities are sometimes hard to see because the piece that causes the stalemate has not yet been created. When your opponent "allows" you to queen a pawn, double-check that he hasn't set you up for a stalemate.

The next example shows a slightly more complicated version of underpromotion. In Diagram 91, White plays **1.f8=Q**, but Black's King is then stalemated. To draw, all Black has to do is give away his Queen: **1...Qe1+ 2.Kg2 Qxg3+!! 3.Kxg3** Stalemate. If White had noticed that promotion to a Queen leads to a draw, he might have played 1.f8=N+! Kh8 2.Bd4+ with checkmate to follow.

Here's another example. White seems to be in big trouble in Diagram 92. If he promotes his pawn to a Queen, then 1...Qh3 is checkmate. Salvation comes in the form of a fork. Underpromoting with **1.f8=N+!** creates a royal fork, and

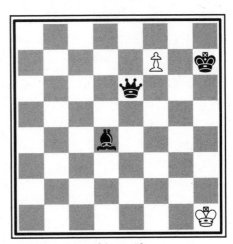

DIAGRAM 92. White to play.

after Black moves his King, **2.Nxe6** captures the Black Queen. The wise player who considers all checks and captures before moving will never miss this sort of move.

The following tests all feature the underpromotion tactic. As usual, these tests get progressively more difficult.

Tests

TEST 74. It's White's move. Is it safe for him to make a Queen?

TEST 75. Again, it's White's turn to play. Can he win this position?

TEST 76. This position is an elegant composition by former World Champion Emanuel Lasker. Like all World Champions, he had a keen eye for tactics, especially underpromotion—a surprising move that seems to defy logic. In this study, Black appears to have the superior position. He is up a piece for two pawns, and White's King is vulnerable to eventual back rank checkmate threats. For example, if Black could play ...Qd7 followed by ...Qd1+, he would win quickly. It's White's move. How can he turn this situation around?

Study by Em. Lasker

CHAPTER NINE

The Decoy

Decoy tactics are some of the most satisfying in chess. The idea is simple: If you find yourself wishing that one of your opponent's pieces were on a particular square, you must find a way to force him to move there. To perform this magic, it's often useful to visualize the position you want and then do your best to create it (always bearing in mind that your opponent will not willingly cooperate). If achieving your goal involves a sacrifice, then so be it. Naturally, the sacrifice is the prettiest kind of decoy. However, some other enticement will often do the trick.

Diagram 93 shows a simple example of a nonsacrificial decoy. White would love Black's g-pawn to move so that the f6-Bishop is no longer defended. So White plays **1.Qf5**, threatening checkmate on h7. Black can save his King only with **1...g6**, but then White's wish is fulfilled because **2.Qxf6** wins the Bishop.

Notice that 1.Qh5 would also threaten checkmate but would lead to nothing after 1...g6. What would you play after 1...h6 in reply to 1.Qh5? In general, any move that threatens checkmate is worth considering and, if you are lucky enough to have more than one move, be sure you choose the best of the lot!

That example was easy! A sacrificial decoy is much more fun. Our next four examples all demonstrate this kind of decoy tactic.

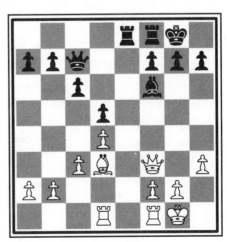

DIAGRAM 93. White to play.

DIAGRAM 94. White to play.   DIAGRAM 95. Black to play.

White is putting some pressure on Black's c-pawn in Diagram 94, but at the moment, the pawn appears to be well defended by Black's Queen and Rook. Now take a closer look. Note that the only thing stopping White from playing Qxg7 Checkmate is Black's Queen. Therefore, the Queen cannot really defend the c6-pawn because she must keep a constant eye on the g7-pawn. To win, White need only force Black's Queen away from this critical pawn. Thus, **1.Rxc6!** is an obvious decoy. Black can't capture with 1...Qxc6 because of the threatened 2.Qxg7 Checkmate, but any other Queen move would lead to the loss of Black's Rook on c8.

The position in Diagram 95 has all the characteristics of the previous example. The only thing that prevents ...Qxf2 Checkmate is White's Queen. Black's mission: to lure White's Queen away from the defense of the f2-square. The solution is **1...Ba6!**. This pin presents an immediate threat of 2...Qxf2 Checkmate that cannot be prevented by 2.Qxa6. (The White Queen can't move away because she is in an absolute pin.) Trying to block the Bishop with 2.b5 fails when Black plays 2...Bxb5!, and White's loss solves none of his problems.

In Diagram 96, Black also seems to be well positioned. His Rooks are doubled on the open c-file, and he intends to play ...Bf6, putting pressure on the d4-pawn. White must react quickly. Fortunately, he's able to win material. Though Black's Bishop is defended by a Rook and a Knight, White can destroy one defender with **1.Rxc6!** and simultaneously drag the other defender away from its defense of e7. After **1...Rxc6 2.Rxe7**, White has gained a 1-point advantage in force.

I'll finish this study of the decoy tactic with an example of a piece drawn to a square that it normally wouldn't dream of going to. A quick look at Diagram 97 should be enough to convince you that 1.Qg5?? is a terrible idea because 1...Nh3+ creates a royal fork on White's King and Queen. Experienced players are familiar with forks and would never knowingly walk into one. Of course, that doesn't mean they can't occasionally be lured into a fork! The next position shows just such a case.

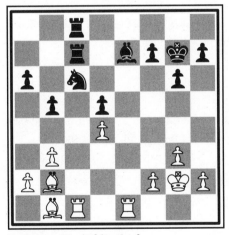

DIAGRAM 96. White to play.

DIAGRAM 97. White to play.

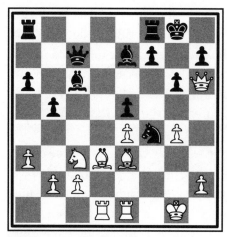

DIAGRAM 98. Black to play.
Paoli–Anderssen
Dortmund, 1973

In Diagram 98, Black forces his opponent to step into the fork just presented in Diagram 97 by playing **1...Bg5!**, after which **2.Qxg5** (the Queen had nowhere safe to go) **2...Nh3+** picks off the Queen. White didn't want to move to the g5-square, but the decoy sacrifice left him with no choice. Notice the key role played by the Black Knight on the f4-square. Any time you notice that your Knight is within checking distance of the enemy King, look for favorable ways to "cash the check."

Now solve the following tests by imagining where you would like the opponent's pieces to go and then forcing them to go there.

Tests

Szabo–Bronstein
Zürich, 1953

TEST 77. It's White's move. He sees that he can attack Black's royal family with 1.Qh8+, but after 1...Kf7, the King is able to defend his lady. Can you make White's check on h8 more effective?

TEST 78. This position is from one of the most nerve-racking games of my career. It's my turn to play. My opponent, Perry Youngworth, is winning the US Junior Championship. If I fail to win this game, Perry will be the US representative to the World Junior Championship instead of me. To make matters worse, I am running out of time and have no chance to make a considered decision. I can see that 1...Qf3+ 2.Kg1 Nh3 will be checkmate, but this bit of fantasy is ruined by the obvious 2.Qxf3. How did I get to the World Junior Championships?

Youngworth–Seirawan
Los Angeles, 1979

TEST 79. It's a close game, and it's White's move. Can you find an immediate knockout for White?

Ustinov–Ilivicki
USSR, 1959

TEST 80. It's Black's turn to play, and his position is grim. The unstoppable threat of Qxg7 Checkmate hangs over him like a dark cloud. "If only my Bishop were on f3," moans Black to himself, "then I could call the shots with ...Rd1 Checkmate." How can Black create the winning position?

Seitz–Rellstab
Bad Pyrmont, 1933

Clearance Sacrifice

Imagine this situation: You have an opportunity to make a big move—a move that's strong enough to win material or perhaps even checkmate. The catch is that one of your own pieces is in the way, and taking the time to move the obstruction to a safe square will give your opponent the chance to mount a defense.

The solution to this dilemma is to sacrifice the obstructing piece! Known as a *clearance sacrifice*, this tactic forces your opponent to take the obstructing piece, thereby vacating the square of your dreams and forestalling any defensive measures.

How can you force your opponent to capture the piece, even though this action will lead to his doom? The best way is to check your opponent's King with the obstructing piece, which forces a response. The next best way is to capture something with the obstructing piece. If your opponent does not recapture, you will have gained a material advantage.

Obviously, a checking move is the most compelling method. An example is shown in Diagram 99, where White is mounting a strong attack down the g-file. If his Rook were not on g7, he could make a brilliant checkmate with Qg7. The problem here is to dump the obstructing Rook and clear the g7-square, without giving Black the time

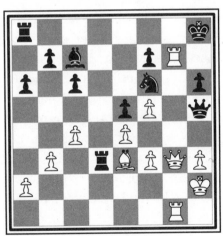

DIAGRAM 99. White to play.
Lisitsin–Zagoriansky
USSR, 1936

DIAGRAM 100. White to play.

to stop the desired checkmate. Because 1.Rg8+?? fails to 1...Rxg8 and 1.Rxf7 Qxf7 allows Black to defend the g7-square, White must find a more forcing variation. This is where the check comes in. White plays **1.Rh7+!**. Black must take the Rook but has no time to stop the checkmate— **1...Kxh7 2.Qg7** Checkmate.

The next example also involves a checkmating situation, but this time the solution is a bit more complex. In Diagram 100, both Kings are in terrible trouble. Black threatens to checkmate on a2, and defenses like 1.Rd2 fail to 1....Qxa2+! 2.Rxa2 Rxa2 Checkmate. Clearly White has to get to Black's King first. White notices that if the White Queen were not on f5, he could play the powerful Nf5+. Checks are the only threats that will keep Black from dropping the axe, so White moves his Queen out of the way with a forcing check: **1.Qxg5+!**. The f5-square is now vacant, and Black must take the White Queen with **1...Nxg5**, which leads to **2.Nf5+ Kg6 3.h5** Checkmate. This series of checks prevents Black from making the one move he needed to win the game.

Our goal in Diagrams 99 and 100 was checkmate. However, at times the target will be a piece other than the enemy King. In Diagram 101, the Black Queen has few moves. If former World Champion Mikhail Botvinnik can play Nc4, he will attack the Queen, cover the b6-square, and unleash his g3-Bishop on the c7-square. In other words, the Black Queen will be trapped! The problem is that the c4-square is occupied by a White Bishop. Bearing in mind what you have just learned about the clearance sacrifice, you'll easily understand the moves of this great World Champion: **1.Bxf7+!** (vacating the c4-square for White's Knight) **1...Rxf7 2.Nc4**. Black loses his Queen and eventually loses the game.

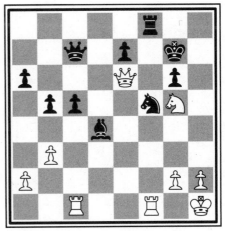

DIAGRAM 101. White to play.
Botvinnik–Stepanov
USSR, 1931

DIAGRAM 102. White to play.
Tal–Parma
Bled, 1961

The "Wizard of Riga," former World Champion Mikhail Tal, was noted for his bold and imaginative play. His tactical ability was legendary. For example, in 1988, Canadian Senior Master Jonathan Berry served as an International Arbiter at a big international tournament in Saint John, New Brunswick, in which Tal took part. Berry recalls:

> Tal was wandering around the tournament hall looking at games. It just so happened that his path took him past two strong International Masters, who, in mutual time trouble, had agreed upon a draw. Hardly breaking stride, Tal bent, pointed out a sparkling win for one side, smiled, and moved on.

In Diagram 102, Tal is ahead only the Exchange for a pawn—a 1-point edge—and would love to pad his advantage with more material. He realizes that if White's Queen were not on e6, he would be able to launch a maiming royal fork with Ne6+. For a tactical genius like Tal, the solution is obvious: **1.Qxf5!**. With this one move, he clears the e6-square and devours a Knight at the same time. Black resigns rather than face 1...gxf5 2.Ne6+ Kg6 3.Nxc7, after which the material disparity would be too great for him to hope of catching up.

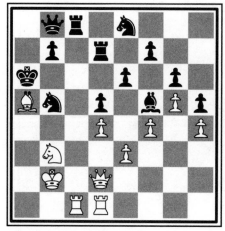

DIAGRAM 103. White to play.

The clearance sacrifice creates unusual situations that sometimes seem to defy chess logic. Normally pieces are valuable, and you go out of your way to shepherd and guard them. But playing a clearance sacrifice allows you to boldly move the obstructing piece wherever you want, without caring whether it's captured or not. You're not concerned about the piece, but rather about controlling the square that it stands on.

The position in Diagram 103 is a good illustration of a move that appears suicidal, yet leads to victory. White has sacrificed a piece and a pawn in order to attack the Black King. If the White Bishop were not on a5, White could win with Qa5 Checkmate. A simple move like 1.Bd8 gets the Bishop out of the way but allows Black to defend with 1...b6. White needs to clear the a5-square with a double attack. He plays **1.Bc7**, moving to a square that is defended no less than five times! Unfortunately for Black, taking the Bishop with his Knights or Rooks makes 2.Qa5 Checkmate possible, and if he plays 1...Qxc7, then 2.Rxc7 ends the game. Black's best move is **1...b6**, even though **2.Bxb8** gives White a decisive advantage in material.

Let's try a few tests. To solve these problems, keep in mind that one of your pieces is in the way of another. Figure out what the obstruction is and then find the most forceful move to clear it out of the way!

Tests

TEST 81. It's Black's turn to play, and White's Bishop is the target. Here's a hint: Look for a fork. Good luck!

Prohorovic–Ravinski
USSR, 1958

TEST 82. White has a forced checkmate possibility, but one of his pieces is in the way. Which one is it, and how can he get rid of it?

Ivkov–Portisch
Bled, 1961

TEST 83. Playing 1.Nh6 produces checkmate, but White isn't allowed to capture his own Queen. How can he force Black to do it for him?

Roneat–Reicher
Germany, 1950

CHAPTER ELEVEN

X-Rays and Windmills

In this chapter, I cover x-rays and windmills, two tactics that lead to surprise attacks. Both are easy to overlook. The x-ray happens fairly often, so you should study it carefully. The windmill is very rare but very powerful: It can lead to the capture of your opponent's entire army!

The X-Ray

The x-ray tactic, which has a lot in common with the discovered attack, brings to mind Superman's ability to see through objects. It enables a piece to mount an attack even when other pieces are in the way. It also enables a piece to capture a defended piece or pawn even when the attacking piece itself doesn't seem to be defended. Only Queens, Rooks, and Bishops can perform an x-ray.

Diagram 104 shows a simple illustration. White has just moved his pawn to a5, attacking the Black Knight. White thinks his pawn is safe because his Rook on c5 protects it. However, in this case, safety turns out to be only an illusion. With **1...Rxa5!**, the a8-Rook captures the pawn, while Black's Rook on d5 applies an x-ray. (The pawn was actually attacked by both Black Rooks, and White's c5-Rook was helpless to stop them.)

The x-ray tactic is particularly strong in the presence of a back rank

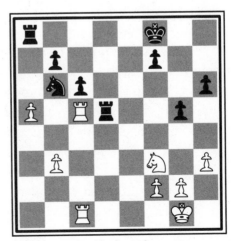

DIAGRAM 104. **Black to play.**

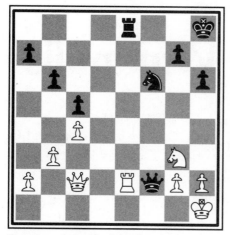
DIAGRAM 105. Black to play.

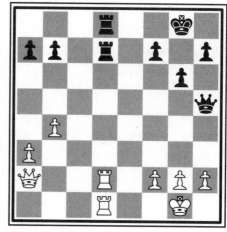
DIAGRAM 106. Black to play.

weakness because threats of check or checkmate then add fuel to its fire. In Diagram 105, White is aware that his King faces the danger of a back rank checkmate, but because the e1- and f1-squares seem well defended, he feels secure. White expects 1...Rxe2 2.Qxe2 to produce an even exchange of material. He fails to perceive that an impending x-ray exists and that the e1-square is attacked not only by Black's Queen but also by his Rook. White's death is swift but sure: **1...Qe1+! 2.Rxe1 Rxe1+ 3.Nf1 Rxf1** Checkmate.

Here's another example of what happens when a player is not aware of an impending x-ray. In Diagram 106, White thinks his Rooks are well protected and expects Black to play the boring 1...Rxd2 2.Rxd2 Rxd2 3.Qxd2. Instead, his universe comes to an end after **1...Qxd1+! 2.Rxd1 Rxd1** Checkmate. Even if White had prevented the back rank checkmate by moving one of his pawns to h3 or g3 earlier, Black would still use the x-ray tactic because he wins two Rooks for a Queen—a 1-point advantage. How could White have avoided this disaster? The wise player considers all the checks and captures at his opponent's disposal, and 1...Qxd1+ is both a check and a capture!

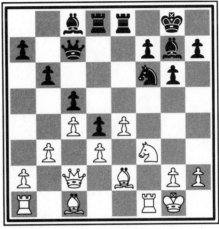

DIAGRAM 107. Black to play.

So far we have looked at pure x-ray attacks. However, some discovered attacks are also x-rays, and it is a toss-up whether they should be discussed here or in Chapter Two, where I covered discovered attacks. Diagram 107 is a case in point. At a glance, you can't tell that Black's Bishop on g7 poses a real threat to White's Rook on a1. Perhaps the Bishop could x-ray through to the Rook, but using this tactic seems more fantasy than reality because the Bishop's diagonal is blocked by a Knight and the solidly entrenched d4-pawn. Black is not deterred by all this sensible thinking, however. He plays **1...Nxe4! 2.dxe4 d3!** (a double attack) **3.Bxd3 Bxa1.** The Black Bishop dines on the White Rook after all!

Notice that Black accomplishes his goal in Diagram 107 by using what we call *forcing moves*. The chief characteristic of these moves is that the opponent's choice of replies is severely limited, which, among other things, makes calculating the likely response much easier.

Tests

TEST 84. It's Black's move. Are any x-rays hiding out here?

TEST 85. Black plays the brazen **1...Nxd3**. Can he get away with this move?

The Windmill

The windmill, an extremely potent but rare tactic, consists of a discovered check, followed by a normal check, followed by a discovered check, and so forth. It ends only when the attacker gets what he wants out of the situation.

In Diagram 108, we see how the windmill tactic enables White to win *everything*. A mixture of checks, discovered checks, and captures leaves Black paralyzed. He is being eaten alive, and there's nothing he can do about it! White begins with **1.Rxd7+**. (Notice that the Bishop on e5 has discovered an attack on Black's King.) Play continues with **1...Kg8 2.Rg7+** (forcing the King back into the same unfortunate discovered-check situation) **2...Kh8 3.Rxc7+ Kg8 4.Rg7+ Kh8 5.Rxb7+ Kg8** (back and forth) **6.Rg7+ Kh8 7.Rxa7+ Kg8 8.Rxa8+**. Black is left with nothing but his King!

Diagram 109 shows one of the most famous uses of the windmill tactic. In this game, Black is the great former World Champion Emanuel Lasker, who held the title for 27 years. If this guy can get caught in a windmill, then everyone is susceptible! White begins with **1.Bf6!**, attacking

DIAGRAM 108. White to play.

the g7-pawn with both the Bishop and the Rook. Black would normally defend with ...Ng6, but 1.Bf6 also uncovers an attack against Black's Queen by her counterpart on h5. So Black reluctantly plays **1...Qxh5**. Now White can use the windmill tactic: **2.Rxg7+ Kh8 3.Rxf7+ Kg8 4.Rg7+ Kh8 5.Rxb7+ Kg8 6.Rg7+ Kh8 7.Rg5+** (here White plays to regain his sacrificed Queen, avoiding 7.Rxa7+ because the Rook on a8 is defended and because, in the long run, opening the a-file would only help Black) **7...Kh7 8.Rxh5.**

DIAGRAM 109. White to play.
Torre–Em. Lasker
Moscow, 1925.

Now White wins without difficulty. Notice that though windmill combinations are quite long, they are rather easy once you get started because play is so forced.

Tests

TEST 86. At the moment, White is down a piece and two pawns. It's his move. How can he turn this game around?

Poletayev–Flohr
Moscow, 1951

TEST 87. In this game, White plays the very strong **1.Qg4**, threatening both 2.Qxd1 and 2.Qxg7+. Black resigns. Can you see another winning tactic for White?

CHAPTER TWELVE

Zwischenzug

I've often been told that chess is a difficult sport for Americans because the language of chess is so "European." Not only do chess players fling around terms like *zugzwang*, *en passant*, and *en prise*, but the names of the players are such tongue twisters. Names like Dzindzihashvili, Nimzovich, and Ljubojevic make the game even harder to grasp. Like any other sport, chess takes practice. In time, terms that once seemed so foreign will become second nature, and the names will roll off your tongue like those of your friends. Soon you'll be adding your own jargon to the body of classic chess terms.

Take the zwischenzug tactic, for example. *Zwischenzug* is a German word that means *an in-between move*. In American parlance, zwischenzug has become *intermezzo* (intermediate), *zwishy*, and the like.

The idea behind a zwischenzug is straightforward. Imagine you are considering initiating a sequence of exchanges that you expect to go something like this: "I capture, he captures, I capture, he captures, and then I win a pawn." Sounds good, doesn't it? So you proceed with your idea, and it comes out like this: "I capture, he captures, I capture, he plays check? OK, no problem. I simply move my King. Oh, oh. Now he captures with a check! Oops." What happened? You are the victim of a zwischenzug. Your opponent sneaked in a move before the anticipated recapture. Lawyers say you should never ask a witness a question if you don't already know the answer. Well, zwischenzugs are the unexpected retorts of chess. Usually (but not always), zwischenzugs are checks.

DIAGRAM 110. Black to play.

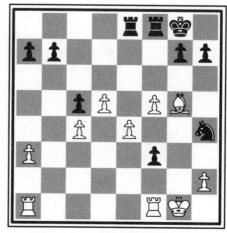

DIAGRAM 111. Black to play.

Diagram 110 shows a zwischenzug in its most basic form. Black is very happy with his position. A pawn ahead, he is anxious to trade pieces and push his a-pawn toward coronation. Overlooking a zwischenzug, Black confidently plays **1...Rxh4** expecting 2.Qxh4 f6, which leaves the a-pawn ready to speed down the board. Instead, White plays **2.Qd8+! Kh7 3.Qxh4+**. The havoc wreaked by the zwischenzug is obvious. White has recaptured with check, and with the safety of his King at stake, Black doesn't have time for 2...f6. After **3...Kg8 4.Qd8+ Kh7**, White can claim a perpetual check with **5.Qh4+**. Alternatively, 5.Qxa5 snaps off the a-pawn.

Zwischenzugs aren't always this straightforward. At the highest levels of chess mastery, zwischenzugs can be much more subtle, with their effects revealed only several moves later. Diagram 111 shows a zwischenzug in a more crafty setting. Black commences a series of exchanges: **1...Rxe4 2.Bxh4 Rxh4 3.Rxf3 Rxc4 4.Re1 Rg4+** (the zwischenzug) **5.Kf2 Rd4 6.Re7 Rxd5 7.Rxb7 Rdxf5 8.Rxf5 Rxf5+**. By recapturing with check, Black gains time, thus maintaining his advantage. Without the zwischenzug, White wouldn't be in check, and he'd have time to capture the a7-pawn.

CHAPTER THIRTEEN

Other Kinds of Draws

Nobody can win every game, and sometimes things will go so badly that a draw would be a wonderful result under the circumstances. Aside from the possibility of a stalemate or a perpetual check (see Chapter Five), you might have other options for saving the game. In this chapter, we'll discuss two of these options: perpetual pursuits and fortress building. We'll also look at positions that result in a drawn game because the stronger side has insufficient material to force a win. All of these situations can easily occur and, if you are defending, will often enable you to draw a game that would normally be considered hopeless. The late American Grandmaster Sammy Reshevsky gave this simple advice about the best attitude to take in a seemingly hopeless situation:

Sit tight and hope for a blunder.

It's also useful to put yourself in your opponent's shoes and find the kind of move that you would least like to see if you were in his place.

Perpetual Pursuits

A perpetual pursuit is similar to a perpetual check except that the pursued piece is a Bishop, Knight, Rook, or Queen instead of the King. The idea is simple: If you can limit the movement of a piece and then constantly attack it, your opponent won't be able to launch any action against you because he will need to safeguard his attacked piece by moving it back and forth. This perpetual motion usually leads to a draw because of the three-time repetition rule:

A draw is declared if the identical position is repeated three times.

Let's look at some examples.

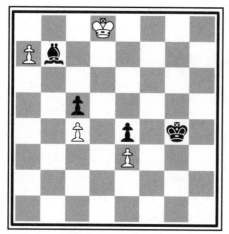 

DIAGRAM 112. White to play.　　DIAGRAM 113. White to play.
　　　　　　　　　　　　　　　　Study by S. Birnov, 1928

In Diagram 112, White is down a piece for a pawn, but he can force a draw by constantly attacking Black's Bishop. After **1.Kc7 Ba8** (Black has nowhere else to run to), White plays **2.Kb8 Bc6 3.Kc7** (avoiding 3.a8=Q Bxa8 4.Kxa8 Kf3 5.Kb7 Kxe3 6.Kc6 Kd4, and Black wins) **3...Ba8 4.Kb8.** At this point, a draw is declared because neither side is getting anywhere and the position will soon be repeated three times.

The position in Diagram 113 is basically the same as that in Diagram 112, except that it can be resolved in a very pleasing way. On the surface, you might expect White to resign. He is down a piece, Black's passed h-pawn is clearly unstoppable, and White's passed a-pawn is easily handled by Black's Bishop. However, White believes in miracles. He begins with **1.a6**, and Black responds with **Bxc4.** (A pawn race would fail for Black because after 1...h3 2.a7 h2 3.a8=Q h1=Q 4.Qxh1, White would win.) Now White makes a superb pawn sacrifice with **2.e4+!**. Black must take this pawn with **2...Kxe4** because he needs to play ...Bd5 to stop White's a-pawn from promoting. Now the Black Bishop's freedom of movement is limited because the Black King sits on the h1–a8 diagonal. Play continues with **3.a7**

Bd5 4.c4!, and White takes another square away from the Bishop. Because 4...Bxc4?? 5.a8=Q+ is unacceptable, Black must run to the a8-square: **4...Ba8 5.Kb8 Bc6 6.Kc7 Ba8 7.Kb8**. The Black Bishop is constantly forced to elude the White King's advances, resulting in a draw by perpetual pursuit.

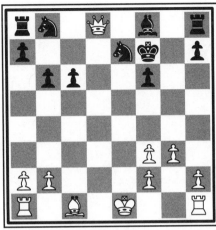

DIAGRAM 114. **Black to play.**

The clever use of the zwischenzug 2.e4+! forced the White King to the e4-square, denying the White Bishop the possibility of retreating back down the h1–a8 diagonal. Sometimes it's useful to mentally insert forcing moves into each possible slot in a series to see which one is most effective. Note that 1.e4+? would not have worked for White because Black can play 1...Ke5! 2.a6 Bh7 3.a7 Bxe4, and the Bishop stops the White a-pawn. A lovely study!

The piece that is most vulnerable to constant attack is the Queen. Virtually every enemy piece can threaten her, and she is simply too valuable to give up. Diagram 114 shows a Queen running for cover only to find that she has no truly safe place to hide. White, who is up a Queen and a pawn for two Knights, seems to be well on his way to victory. However, his fortunes undergo a radical reversal after **1...Nd5!**, when Black threatens to capture the Queen with ...Bb4+ followed by ...Rxd8. White avoids the Bishop's check with **2.0-0**. Now Black is able to force a perpetual pursuit of the Queen with **2...Bg7** (threatening 3...Rxd8) **3.Qd6** (the only safe square) **3...Bf8!** **4.Qd8** (again, the only safe square) **4...Bg7**. Black repeats the position and claims a draw.

Now try your hand at a test. To solve this problem, all you have to do is find something to attack and never let up!

Tests

TEST 88. In this well-known position from the Slav Defense (1.d4 d5 2. c4 c6—one of Black's most solid defenses to the Queen's Gambit), White can capture a "free" pawn on b7 with 1.Qxb7. If White wants to win the game, is capturing this pawn a wise decision?

Building a Fortress

Building a fortress involves setting up a strong defensive wall that prevents your opponent from making decisive inroads into your position. We'll look at two types of walls: one that prevents the King from crossing over into your territory and one that keeps out your opponent's entire army.

Keeping Out the King

When you and your opponent have traded most of your pieces, your best bet is to bring your King into play. No longer attacked by the entire enemy army, his Majesty can show that he is a strong piece in his own right.

A good exercise to test the King's powers against other pieces is to put a monarch on the board against a single enemy Queen or a lone Rook. The best the mighty Queen can do by herself is force a stalemate position. The Rook can set up an impassable wall of squares but that's all. Against a lone Bishop or Knight, the King can also go pretty much where he wants.

The King's strength is particularly apparent when a King and Queen face a lone King or a King and Rook face a lone King. By itself, a Queen or Rook cannot force a checkmate. Both need the King's help. It stands to reason, then, that when you are down material in an endgame, you might be able to save the game if you can keep the enemy King away from your own monarch.

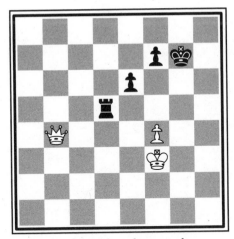

DIAGRAM 115. Either player to play.   DIAGRAM 116. Black to play.

In Diagram 115, White is ahead a Queen for a Rook and a pawn—a 3-point advantage. However, he can't win because his King can't cross over the 5th rank. If his King could get to e7, White would be able to combine an attack against the f7-pawn with an attack against the Black King, winning the game. Black prevents this slaughter by playing ...Rf5–d5–f5–d5. He counters any Queen checks with ...Kg8 or ...Kf8, giving White no way to get his King into the game.

Here, the Rook's power to set up an impassable wall of squares in front of the enemy King has saved the day. Though the Rook has less strength than the Queen, Black draws easily. Substitute a Rook and Knight for the White Queen and see for yourself. This type of anti-King blockade has enabled many a player to save an otherwise hopeless position.

White is very happy with the position in Diagram 116. He is up a Queen and a pawn for a Rook and a Bishop—a 2-point advantage. He intends to answer 1...exd5 with the nasty surprise 2.Qb2+, forking Black's King and Bishop. However, Black sees a chance to create the blockade shown in Diagram 115 and calmly plays **1...Bxd5!**. After **2.exd5 Rxd5**, White will eventually be forced to accept a draw.

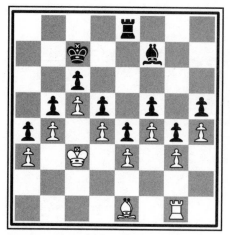

DIAGRAM 117. Either player to move.

DIAGRAM 118. White to play.
Study by V. Chekhover, 1947

Keeping Out the Enemy Army

When you are behind in force, it is very hard to keep all your opponent's pieces out of your camp. However, if you can hold them at bay, then a material imbalance becomes unimportant.

A glance at Diagram 117 is all you need to realize that neither player's army can break into the other's camp. To prove the point, remove Black's Bishop and Rook. Now Black is down 8 full points in force, but he will still draw the game with ease because even with extra forces, White can't do anything to break through.

In Diagram 118, White is doing fine materially (three pawns and a Bishop for a Rook), but Black threatens to play ...Rh2 and then systematically devour all the White pawns. White can force a draw by setting up a blockade that prevents both Black's King and Rook from penetrating White's position. Here's how: **1.Kd1! Rh2 2.Ke1!** (sacrificing the White Bishop) **2...Rxg2 3.Kf1 Rh2 4.Kg1** (kicking the Black Rook out of the White camp) **4...Rh6 5.f3!** White's fifth move is the key to keeping out the Black King. (To test the strength of this move, try to find a way for the Black King to get in.) Play continues with **5...Re6** (Black hopes to get to e2 or e1) **6.Kf1** (protecting the e2- and e1-squares) **6...Kf7 7.Kf2**. Now neither Black's Rook nor his King can penetrate the blockade. White's King will simply shuttle back and forth between f1 and f2. If Black plays ...Rh6, then White's King will switch the action to g1 and g2. Note also that White will counter a Black move of ...a5 and ...a4 with the blocking b4. Thus, the game is an inevitable draw.

In the following tests, simply aim to keep the bad guys out, and all will be well.

Tests

TEST 89. White is up a Queen and pawn for a Rook and a Knight—a 2-point edge. Is 1.e4 a good move for White?

TEST 90. Black is up a Rook, and it's White's turn to play. Should White give up, or can you find a move that offers him a glimmer of hope?

Study by J. Hasek, 1932

Material Imbalances That Lead to a Draw

A material advantage is wonderful but will do you no good if you can't win the game. To become proficient at chess, you must understand that some types of material advantages are not by themselves enough to force a win. If you have a material advantage, you need to know whether it's one of the winning types, and conversely, if you are down material, you need to know whether to try to draw an otherwise lost game. In this section, we'll look at the most common types of non-winning material advantages: two Knights vs. a lone King; a Knight and a Rook-pawn on the 7th vs. a lone King; and a Bishop and a wrong-color Rook-pawn vs. a lone King.

Two Knights vs. a Lone King

One of the greatest injustices of chess is the fact that without pawns on the board, two Knights cannot beat a lone King. Because two Bishops or a Bishop and a Knight can easily accomplish this feat, two Knights are considered less valuable than two Bishops or a Bishop and a Knight. Let's look at the examples in Diagrams 119 and 120.

DIAGRAM 119. White to play.

DIAGRAM 120. Black to play.

In Diagram 119, White is up two Knights for nothing, and he has managed to corner the Black King. But he still can't win the game! If White plays **1.Nh6+**, Black must avoid 1...Kh8?? 2.Ngf7 Checkmate and play **1...Kf8**, which leaves White with no way to kill off the Black King.

Black looks like he is on his last legs in Diagram 120. His King is in trouble, and he is down two pawns. However, Black knows that White's two lone Knights are insufficient for a win, so he plays **1...Nxd5! 2.Kxd5** (2.e7 Nxe7 produces a draw) **2...Nxe6!**. The frustrated commander of the White army can play on for a while, but eventually he must concede the draw.

A Knight and a Rook-Pawn on the 7th vs. a Lone King

If you are ahead in an endgame, the least-valuable pawn to own is usually an a- or h-pawn. In fact, these pawns can be liabilities. Because the a- and h-pawns occupy the edge of the board, they offer the defender stalemate chances that no other pawn would give him.

One such case is the hopeless situation shown in Diagram 121. Black is down a Knight and a pawn. Normally this position would give White an easy win: 1.Kf6 Kg8 2.Kg6 Kh8 3.Nf7+ Kg8 4.h7+, and the pawn is promoted. However, suppose White blunders with **1.h7??**. Suddenly the game is a draw! Though this move would be a winner with any other pawn, here two factors combine to save Black: First, the Black King can't step off the edge of the board; and second, the Knight can't move without hanging the h-pawn, and if the White King defends the h-pawn, a stalemate will occur. After **1... Kg7 2.Kf5 Kh8**, the direct **3.Kf6** produces an immediate stalemate, and **3.Kg4 Kg7 4.Kh5 Kh8** gets White nowhere because **5.Kh6** still stalemates the Black King.

DIAGRAM 121. White to play.

DIAGRAM 122. Black to play.

Diagram 122 shows another example. Though down a pawn, Black draws easily by playing for the position in the previous diagram. With **1...Nf5!**, he forces White's pawn to the unfortunate h7-square. White obliges: **2.h7 Nd4 3.Kd1 Nxc2!** (the simple 3...Kg7 also draws, but Black wants to be dramatic) **4.Kxc2 Kg7 5.Kxc3 Kh8**. Now White simply can't win.

The moral of all these positions is simply this:

If you are way ahead in material and you have an a- or h-pawn, be careful not to give your opponent a chance for a stalemate!

A Bishop and a Wrong-Color Rook-Pawn vs. a Lone King

Forcing a stalemate with this combination of material is probably the most useful last-minute saving technique a defending player has. This situation comes up amazingly often. The attacking player is confident of his extra material and often fails to notice this defensive possibility until too late.

The position in Diagram 123 is a simple illustration of this theme. The result will be a draw no matter where the pawn sits on the h-file. If White's Bishop stood on the dark squares, White would win easily, but the fact that the pawn promotes on the color opposite to that of the Bishop enables Black to hold on by taking advantage of the stalemating possibilities offered by the a- or h-pawn. After **1.Kg6 Kg8 2.h7+ Kh8**, White is faced with a stalemate (as he also is with 2.Be6+ Kh8). No matter what White does, he will be unable to chase Black out of his corner.

The vintage position in Diagram 124 shows that this method of defending against a Bishop and a wrong-color Rook-pawn has been known for a very long time! Black saves himself with **1...Ra1+ 2.Rf1 Rxf1+ 3.Kxf1 Bh3! 4.gxh3**. White would like to play 4.g3, but his pawn is pinned to his

DIAGRAM 123. White to play.

DIAGRAM 124. Black to play.

King! Also notice that 4.Kf2 Bxg2! leads to the position shown in the previous diagram. With **4...Kh6**, Black retreats to his corner on h8 and claims the draw. No matter how many pawns White piles up on the h-file, the game will end in a draw unless the White Bishop controls the pawns' queening square.

The drawing mechanism we have just looked at is very useful and should be studied thoroughly. Whenever you are losing and your opponent has a Bishop and a Rook-pawn of the wrong color, there is still hope!

Trapping the Big Gun

Another way to save a game if you are down in material is to trap your opponent's strongest piece and make it more or less useless. Remember, if it can't flex its muscles, it can't cause you any pain.

In Diagram 125 on the next page, Black is up a Rook for a mere pawn. However, White can save himself by entombing the Rook with **1.Bb8!**. Now the only active participants in the game are the two Kings and Black's Bishop. Because a lone Bishop can't force a win, the game must eventually end in a draw.

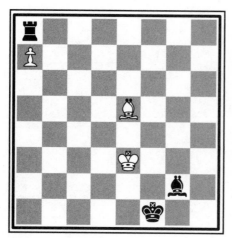

DIAGRAM 125. White to play.

DIAGRAM 126. White to play.
Study by F. Zimkhovitch, 1927

Diagram 126 shows a complicated but extremely beautiful example of how to nullify the powers of the strongest piece on the board. The trouble with White's game is his very weak b2-pawn. Black threatens to win with ...Rb1 and ...Rxb2, when Black's b-pawn would rush down the board and become a Queen. White first takes steps to prevent the promotion: **1.Bg4+ Kd6 2.Bf5! Ra2!** (threatening to get the pawn after all) **3.Nxa2!**. White captures the Rook, but now the Black b-pawn turns into an unstoppable a-pawn with **3...bxa2 4.Kc1 a1=Q+**. However, after **5.Bb1!**, White is assured of a draw. Though Black is ahead a full Queen for a Bishop—a 6-point advantage—he can't win because his Queen has no moves. She's on the board but has no role in the game. White will play Kc2–c1–c2 ad infinitum, until Black agrees to the draw.

Now for a couple of tests. In the following diagrams, you are down and quickly losing consciousness, but in every case you can find a way to hold on. Many a player would be depressed by these positions, but with a positive attitude and a little knowledge, you can often work miracles.

130

Tests

TEST 91. Black is down two pawns and threatened with f6+. It's his move. How can he wipe the smile off White's face?

TEST 92. Black is down two pawns and being pushed backward. Should Black resign; break down sobbing and beg for mercy; or show that he is a real genius?

PART 2

Great Tacticians and Their Games

Whenever chess aficionados get together and the discussion turns to one great player or another, the question of his playing style always comes up. Was that chess master a quiet positional player who enjoyed maneuvering his pieces to and fro? Or was he a madman who turned the board into a minefield of tactical possibilities? This part is dedicated to players of the latter type: the men considered to be the greatest tacticians of all time.

CHAPTER FOURTEEN

Adolf Anderssen

(1818–1879)

Born in Breslau, Germany, Adolf Anderssen is considered to be one of the greatest combinative players of all time. In the course of his long tournament and match career, he won the first big international tournament (London, 1851) and was considered to be the strongest player in the world until his defeat in match play by the American Paul Morphy in 1858. He also won first prizes at Manchester in 1862 and Baden-Baden in 1870, took third at Vienna in 1873, and finished sixth at Paris in 1878 at the age of 60.

Like the majority of players of his day, Anderssen knew only how to attack, but in a field crowded with attackers, he had no equal. His two most famous victories—the Immortal Game and the Evergreen Game—will live as long as chess itself. An amazing imagination and unequaled tactical eye make his games exemplary sources of fantasy for which past and present masters have always had a fondness.

In 1877, Anderssen received a very rare honor from German chess players, who organized a tournament to commemorate the 50th anniversary of Anderssen's first chess game. He showed that he had learned the

DIAGRAM 127. White to play.
Anderssen–Zukertort
Berlin, 1869

game well by tying for second and third place in the tournament at the advanced age (for the 19th century) of 59.

The following example shows how Anderssen typically hacked his opponent to bits. In Diagram 127, material is even, but Black's minor pieces are out of the battle and White's pieces and pawns are threatening the Black King. Seeing his chance for a strange sort of back rank checkmate, Anderssen lures Black's King into the open with **1.Qxh7+! Kxh7** (now 2.Rh3+ fails to 2...Qh6, so White prevents Black's Queen from defending) **2.f6+! Kg8** (even more abrupt is 2...Qxd3 3.Rh3+ Kg8 4.Rh8 Checkmate) **3.Bh7+!** (allowing White's Rook to check the King with tempo. The immediate 3.Rh3 allows Black to create an escape route on f7 for his King with 3...Rxf6.) **3...Kxh7 4.Rh3+ Kg8 5.Rh8** Checkmate.

Anderssen played such extraordinary games that some were given the distinction of a title. Two such games were dubbed "The Immortal Game" and "The Evergreen Game."

The Immortal Game
Anderssen-Kieseritzky
London, 1851

Played in London in 1851, this "friendly" game caused a great stir at the time and was reported in newspapers and journals around the world. In 1855, a chess journalist named Karl Falkbeer referred to it as "The Immortal

Game," believing that it would always be one of the greatest chess games ever played. Here it is.

1.e4 e5

2.f4

White's second move is the prelude to a pawn sacrifice known as the *King's Gambit*, an ultra-aggressive opening that was very popular in Anderssen's day. White's idea is to sacrifice a pawn to gain a majority of center pawns, potential open files for his Rooks, and a lead in development. Today, the King's Gambit is rarely seen in top-flight chess.

2...exf4

Like most players of the last century, Black feels duty-bound to accept the sacrifice. It is the "manly" thing to do!

3.Bc4

Modern players prefer 3.Nf3, which prevents Black's next move.

3...Qh4+

4.Kf1 b5?!

This dubious counter-sacrifice drives the Bishop from its nice diagonal but gives up the pawn.

5.Bxb5 Nf6

6.Nf3

Both sides are hurrying to mobilize their pieces for the attack. Here, White develops his Knight with tempo because it attacks the Black Queen.

6...Qh6

7.d3

White defends his e4-pawn and frees his c1-Bishop.

7...Nh5?

This move is typical of the period. Though Black is threatening 8...Ng3+ 9.hxg3 Qxh1+, he is also placing his Knight on the rim, where it loses its influence over the center. In those days, players often brought out two or three pieces and then started to attack. Now players give more thought to controlling the center and the deployment of *all* their forces. By today's standards, Black has violated the principle of not moving the same piece twice in the opening.

8.Nh4

White stops Black's threat, intending to position the Knight on the nice f5 outpost, from which it can harass the Black Queen.

8...Qg5

9.Nf5

Note how both players are moving the same pieces again and again.

9...c6

10.g4 Nf6?

More lost time. Black should have played for an exchange of pieces with 10...cxb5 11.gxh5, even though White would retain an advantage.

11.Rg1!

White has had enough! He defends his g-pawn and sacrifices the Bishop so that his pawns can gain time by chasing Black's Queen.

11...cxb5

Not wishing to be banned from all future chess events, Black reluctantly accepts the gift and glares defiantly at his opponent.

12.h4 Qg6

13.h5 Qg5

14.Qf3

White develops a piece and threatens to play 15.Bxf4, which will trap Black's Queen.

14...Ng8

Black continues to play with this Knight, but now his Queen can safely retreat to f6 or d8.

15.Bxf4

Another White piece comes out with gain of tempo.

15...Qf6

16.Nc3 Bc5?

This attack on White's Rook is easily parried. Black should have realized that preventing White's next move was more important than engaging in a counterattack.

17.Nd5!?

A modern player would push back Black with 17.d4, expecting 17...Be7, after which 18.Nd5 is crushing. If Black plays 17...Bxd4, then 18.Nd5 wins a piece. However, true to his nature, Anderssen jumps forward with reckless abandon. (He probably planned the checkmate on move 23 and couldn't resist the chance to play into it.)

17...Qxb2

Black attacks White's Rook on a1.

18.Bd6! (128)

White ignores all Black's threats. As you can see in Diagram 128, White is starting to surround the Black King with his pieces.

18...Qxa1+

19.Ke2 Bxg1?

Greedy. But Black was duty-bound to chop off the Rook and challenge White to prove his point.

20.e5

A crafty move. White has absolutely no intention of allowing the Black Queen to take part in his opponent's defense.

20...Na6

Black could have put up a much stiffer resistance by playing 20...Ba6, which gives his King the c8-square to run to. Then White gets a winning ending only after 21.Nc7+ Kd8 22.Nxa6 Bb6 23.Qxa8 Qc3 24.Qxb8+ Qc8 25.Qxc8+ Kxc8 26.Bf8 h6

DIAGRAM 128.

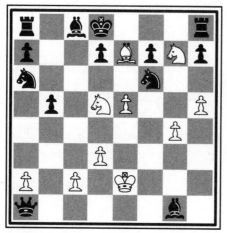

DIAGRAM 129.

27.Nd6+ Kd8 28.Nxf7+ Ke8 29.Nxh8 Kxf8 30.Ng6+ Kf7 31.c3 Ke6 32.d4.

21.Nxg7+ Kd8

22.Qf6+!

White draws the Knight away from the defense of the e7-square.

22...Nxf6

23.Be7 Checkmate

The final position, shown in Diagram 129, is very pleasing! White has sacrificed his Queen, both Rooks, and a Bishop to obtain a pure minor piece checkmate. A pure checkmate is one in which none of the squares around the checkmated King is covered more than once by the winning side. Though obtaining a pure checkmate is more satisfying to composers of chess problems than to over-the-board players, it is fitting that this famous final position has this aesthetic bonus.

The Evergreen Game
Anderssen-Dufresne
Berlin, 1852

Another of Anderssen's "friendly" games was immortalized when Wilhelm Steinitz, the first official World Champion, dubbed it "The Evergreen Game." It went like this:

    1.e4 e5

    2.Nf3 Nc6

    3.Bc4 Bc5

    4.b4

The *Evans Gambit* is another old-time favorite. White sacrifices a pawn so that he can gain time by pushing around Black's Bishop. Modern Grandmasters prefer 4.d3 for a quieter game.

4...Bxb4

5.c3 Ba5

6.d4

Yet another pawn sacrifice. White blows apart the center in the hope that the newly opened lines will provide access to the Black King.

6...exd4

7.0-0 d3

Black loses time because White has no interest in wasting a move to recapture this pawn.

8.Qb3

White eschews recapturing the pawn and threatens 9.Bxf7+, which will win a pawn and check the King.

8...Qf6

Black defends the f7-pawn by placing his Queen on a vulnerable square.

9.e5 Qg6

Black doesn't fall for White's trap and play 9...Nxe5??, which leads to 10.Re1 d6 11.Nxe5 dxe5 12.Qa4+, followed by 13.Qxa5 and the loss of the Black Bishop. Black knows that when your King is in the center, he shouldn't open up any new files.

10.Re1 Nge7

11.Ba3 b5?!

Instead of getting his King to safety with 11...0-0, Black tries to counterattack. He's forgotten the principle that you should avoid opening lines when your King is in the center.

12.Qxb5 Rb8

13.Qa4 Bb6

14.Nbd2 Bb7

15.Ne4 Qf5?

Black continues to waste time and continues to leave his King in the center.

16.Bxd3

White threatens 17.Nd6+, with a discovered attack on Black's Queen.

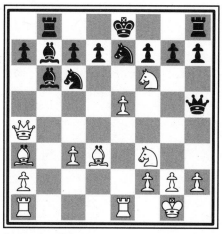

DIAGRAM 130.

16...Qh5

17.Nf6+! (130)

As you can see in Diagram 130, White wants to force Black to capture the Knight on f6. (White will take the Black Queen on h5 if Black resists.) The reason for this sacrifice is that after 18.exf6, White has blasted open the e-file and enabled his Rooks to join in the hunt for Black's King. The possibility of opening lines against the enemy King, especially when he is in the center, should always be considered.

17...gxf6

18.exf6 Rg8

19.Rad1 Qxf3

Black can't resist taking this Knight because he can now threaten to checkmate White on g2.

20.Rxe7+! Nxe7?

After this move, White has a forced checkmate. Black probably overlooked White's stunning reply. I say "probably" because in the old days players who knew they had lost a game sometimes allowed their opponents to win brilliantly. A better defense was 20...Kd8! 21.Rxd7+ Kc8 22.Rd8+! Kxd8 (not 22...Nxd8, which leads to 23.Qd7+!! Kxd7 24.Bf5++ and then Bd7 Checkmate) 23.Bf5+ Qxd1+ 24.Qxd1+ Nd4 25.g3! (which defends the g2-pawn before taking the d4-Knight—the Knight is pinned and will not run away) 25...Bd5 26.cxd4, resulting in a winning position for White.

21.Qxd7+! Kxd7

22.Bf5++

Black's defense won't come easily in the face of a double check.

22...Ke8

If Black tries to escape with 22...Kc6, then 23.Bd7 is checkmate.

23.Bd7+ Kf8

24.Bxe7 Checkmate

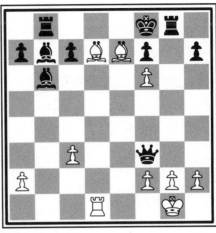

DIAGRAM 131.

Diagram 131 shows the final position. If these two famous games are anything to go by, Anderssen must have been fond of checkmating his opponents by placing a Bishop on e7!

Anderssen's place in chess history is a bit difficult to assess. The author of some of the most famous chess combinations, he lost the two most important matches he ever played. It was a tribute to his standing in the chess world that Paul Morphy was universally considered the strongest player in the world after defeating Anderssen in 1858. After Wilhelm Steinitz edged Anderssen out of the winner's seat with a score of 8–6 in 1866, he claimed to be the first World Champion and was generally accepted to be such. It is worth noting that Anderssen is the man he had to beat to wear this crown.

CHAPTER FIFTEEN

Paul Morphy

(1837–1884)

Born in New Orleans, Louisiana, of a Spanish-Irish father and a French Creole mother, Paul Morphy was an exceptionally strong player by the age of 12. Later he studied law and was said to have been able to recite most of the Civil Code of Louisiana from memory. He passed the bar at 19 and had to wait a year to be eligible to practice law, so he decided to spend some time playing chess. That year—1857—it so happened that the American Chess Congress was held in New York. Morphy's stunning victory at the Congress was followed by a triumphant European tour, culminating in his match win over Anderssen. Morphy returned to the United States in 1859 universally acclaimed as the best player in the world. Sadly, he played no serious chess for the rest of his life and was beset by mental problems in his later years.

Why was Morphy so much better at chess than everyone else? He was a great tactician, but no more so than Adolf Anderssen. What made him invincible was his understanding of some modern chess principles. He attacked only after he had developed all his forces, and he fought like a tiger for control of the center.

The fact that Morphy was ahead of his time was lost on his contemporaries, most of whom could never figure out how he had trampled them under his feet. After losing to Morphy, Anderssen wrote:

> He who plays with Morphy must abandon all hope of catching him in a trap, no matter how cunningly laid, but must assume that it is so clear to Morphy that there can be no question of a false step.

Let's look at one of Morphy's outstanding games.

Morphy–Duke of Braunschweig and Count Isouard, Paris, 1858

In this game, Morphy offered an exquisite example of rapid mobilization of an army followed by flawless execution of an attack. The game was played in a French opera theater and was reported around the world. Though Morphy faced the combined wits of a Duke and a Count, the battle proved to be one-sided. It is considered required reading for all chess lovers. Enjoy.

1.e4 e5

2.Nf3 d6

This opening is the Philidor Defense, named after François-André Danican Philidor (1726–1795). It has the disadvantage of blocking Black's King-Bishop and giving White a free hand in the center.

3.d4

With this move, White opens up diagonals for both his Bishops. Note the speed with which Morphy develops his pieces.

3...Bg4?

A big mistake. Black helps White develop his army.

4.dxe5 Bxf3

Forced. If Black plays 4...dxe5, White responds 5.Qxd8+ Kxd8 6.Nxe5, winning a pawn.

5.Qxf3 dxe5

6.Bc4

White brings out another piece with gain of tempo. Now 7.Qxf7 and checkmate is the threat.

6...Nf6

7.Qb3!

A double attack. White threatens both 8.Bxf7+ and 8.Qxb7, winning a pawn in either case.

7...Qe7

8.Nc3!

A masterful move. After the simple 8.Qxb7 Qb4+ 9.Qxb4 Bxb4+ 10.c3, White would have had a healthy extra pawn and a technical win. Morphy shows admirable restraint and, instead of grabbing Black's b-pawn, decides to go for a quick knockout. This approach requires that he develop his pieces as quickly as possible.

Notice the difference between Morphy and the other players of his era: He attacks only after developing all his pieces, whereas other players bring out one or two men and attack right away. (Another difference is that other players feel obliged to accept all material offers, whereas Morphy accepts them only if doing so gives him an advantage.)

Back to the game.

8...c6

Black defends the b7-pawn and keeps White's pieces out of the d5-outpost.

9.Bg5

White calmly brings out another piece.

9...b5?

Typically, Black tries to solve his problems with a counterattack, but because of White's superior development, such a move is doomed to failure. (Today, everyone knows that an open position always favors the side that is better developed.) Now White has the opportunity to completely open up the position.

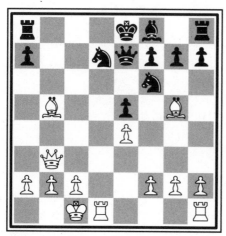

DIAGRAM 132.

10.Nxb5!

With most of his pieces out and his Rooks ready to pounce on the open d-file, White is ready for action.

10...cxb5?

Black accelerates his own defeat. He would be down a pawn after 10...Qb4+ 11.Nc3 Qxb3, but then 12.axb3 creates a winning position for White.

11.Bxb5+ Nbd7

12.0-0-0! (132)

Simultaneously sprinting his King to safety, White puts a Rook on the open d-file. Diagram 132 shows that the pinned d7-Knight is under heavy pressure.

12...Rd8

The f6-Knight is pinned, so the horse on d7 needs additional protection.

13.Rxd7! Rxd7

14.Rd1

White is using all his pieces, whereas Black's f8-Bishop and h8-Rook are playing no part in the game.

14...Qe6

Black tries desperately to slip out of some of the pins.

Now, having marshaled all his men, Morphy finds a pretty and forcing victory.

15.Bxd7+ Nxd7

16.Qb8+! Nxb8

The Black Knight must take White's Queen, allowing White's Rook to deliver the coup de grace.

17.Rd8 Checkmate

A magical game. With simple artistry, Morphy combined strategy and tactics to create this masterpiece.

Other Plays

Only Adolf Anderssen could claim to be Morphy's superior in the realm of tactics, but Anderssen was inferior to Morphy in all other aspects of the game. Lesser mortals were usually bludgeoned to death. A few snapshots from Morphy's career will serve to further demonstrate his tactical skills.

In Diagram 133, White's a1-Rook and b1-Knight are still sitting on their original squares, whereas all of Black's pieces are developed. Morphy shows how to exploit the moment. With **1...Ng3!!**, he puts White's King in a stalemated position and takes advantage of White's unprotected Queen. White can't capture the Knight because 1...Qxe4 wins the White Queen. A response of **2.Qxg6** leads to **2...Nde2** Checkmate.

In Diagram 134, note how Black's pieces work together as a unit and are all placed in or aiming at the center. Because three of White's pieces are sitting uselessly on the Queenside, Black starts an attack against the abandoned White King with **1...Qxf3!!**, a celebrated combination that exposes the King to the fury of the Black Rooks and Bishops. Play continues with **2.gxf3 Rg6+ 3.Kh1 Bh3 4.Rd1** (playing 4.Rg1 instead results in a

DIAGRAM 133. Black to play.
Marache–Morphy
New York, 1857

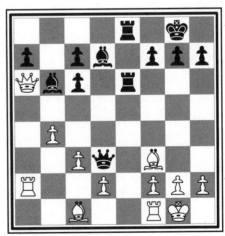

DIAGRAM 134. Black to play.
Paulsen–Morphy
New York, 1857

back rank checkmate: 4...Bg2+! 5.Rxg2 Re1+ 6.Rg1 Rexg1 Checkmate)
4...Bg2+ 5.Kg1 Bxf3+ (avoiding 5...Bh3+ 6.Kh1 Bg2+ 7.Kg1, which results
in a perpetual check and a draw—Morphy wants victory) **6.Kf1 Bg2+.**
Black has no intention of taking White's Rook because doing so would give
White the time to organize a defense. However, he would have done better
to play 6...Rg2! 7.Qd3 Rxf2+ 8.Kg1 Rg2+ 9.Kf1 or Kh1 Rg1 Checkmate. As it
is, the game continues with **7.Kg1 Bh3+.** Black is getting lazy. He could
have finished the game off with either 7...Bf3+, transposing back to the
previously explained sequence, or 7...Be4+ 8.Kf1 Bf5 9.Qe2 Bh3+ 10.Ke1 Rg1
Checkmate. White now plays **8.Kh1 Bxf2** (threatening 9...Bg2 Checkmate)
9.Qf1 Bxf1 10.Rxf1 Re2 11.Ra1 Rh6 12.d4 Be3, whereupon White
resigns. He has no desire to see 13.Bxe3 Rhxh2+ 14.Kg1 Reg2 Checkmate.

CHAPTER SIXTEEN

Rudolf Spielmann

(1883–1942)

Rudolf Spielmann was a short, mild-mannered, and friendly man. Like Adolf Anderssen, Spielmann's personality had little to do with his chess style, which was recklessly aggressive. Unlike Anderssen, however, Spielmann did not play chess in the Romantic era, and defensive technique had become more important. Positional concepts, rather than exclusively combinational ideas, were the stock-in-trade of the masters of Spielmann's day. Crazed, attacking players were looked upon as relics from an earlier, more primitive time.

A lover of gambit openings, Spielmann played many swashbuckling games but never felt that he had reached his full potential. Finally, in the late 1920s, Spielmann undertook a thorough study of positional concepts and endgames. The resulting change of style propelled him into the ranks of the world's top ten players. Reuben Fine once wrote that Spielmann's main concern in life, apart from chess, was to accumulate enough money to buy limitless quantities of beer!

Always proud of his attacking prowess, Spielmann once lamented, "I can see combinations as well as Alekhine, but I cannot get to the positions where they are possible!" This innocent little statement is actually quite revealing and illustrates the changes the game was undergoing at the time. Of course, you could still sacrifice pieces and attack, but to be successful against the strongest players, you had to master all phases of the game. The time of the one-punch knock-out artist was quickly coming to an end. However, we can still enjoy replaying some haymaker chess games. Let's look at a beautiful example from the young Spielmann. His beloved beer must have tasted good after this one!

Spielmann–A. Flamberg
Mannheim, 1914

This game is a good example of Spielmann's early style.

1.e4 e5

2.Nc3 Nf6

3.f4

This part of the Vienna Opening was a great favorite of Spielmann's early in his career.

3...d5

4.fxe5 Nxe4

5.Nf3 Bg4

Today's theorists recommend 5...Be7 because it gives Black equality.

6.Qe2 Nc5

7.d4 Bxf3?

Black thinks he is forcing a trade of Queens, but he is really handing White the kind of opportunity for attack that Spielmann dreamed about. Black should have played 7...Ne6, giving White only a small advantage.

8.Qxf3 Qh4+

9.g3!

Black expected 9.Qf2, leading to a trade of Queens. But Spielmann has no compunctions about sacrificing a couple of pawns for a lead in development and a subsequent attack.

9...Qxd4

10.Be3! Qxe5

11.0-0-0

While Black's Queen is busy snacking on pawns, White rushes to bring out all his pieces.

11...c6

12.Nxd5! (135)

As Diagram 135 shows, this piece sacrifice opens up all the central files to Black's King.

12...cxd5

13.Rxd5 Qe6?

Confused, Black makes a mistake and goes down fast. The best defense, 13...Qc7, still gives White a winning attack after 14.Bb5+ because of his commanding lead in development.

14.Bc4

White threatens the simple 15.Bxc5, as well as 15.Rd8+ and 16.Bxe6 with a discovered attack and capture of Black's Queen.

14...Qe4

15.Bxc5!

Black resigns. White's last move is a killing blow, and Black recognizes that 15...Qxf3 16.Re1+ Be7 17.Rxe7+ Kf8 18.Rd8 Checkmate is a gruesome end.

DIAGRAM 135.

Spielmann–R. L'Hermet
Magdeburg, 1927

The next game, played some years later, shows how Spielmann changed his openings. As you'll see, he still loved to attack, but he would usually play a solid opening before showing any aggression.

1.e4 e6

2.d4 d5

Black's first two moves bring about the French Defense.

3.Nd2 dxe4

4.Nxe4 Nd7

5.Nf3 Ngf6

6.Nxf6+ Nxf6

7.Bd3

This is a nice solid variation of the French Defense. Black should play for a quick 7...c5 and a counterattack in the center.

7...h6?

This lemon loses time and gives White a target for an eventual g2–g4–g5 pawn storm on the Kingside. This target is especially tempting if Black decides to castle on the Kingside.

8.Qe2 Bd6

9.Bd2 0-0

10.0-0-0 Bd7

11.Ne5

The mature Spielmann calmly brings all his forces to the center before starting his attack.

11...c5

This counter comes too late. White is well prepared to take advantage of the open lines.

12.dxc5! Bxe5

Not a happy move for Black, but 12...Bxc5 13.g4! would give White a very strong attacking position.

13.Qxe5 Bc6

14.Bf4 Qe7

15.Qd4 Rfd8

16.Bd6 Qe8

17.Rhg1 b6

18.Qh4

White brings his Queen to the Kingside and steps out of the pin on the d-file.

18...bxc5

19.Be5!

Refusing to be tempted by the c5-pawn, White signals with this move that he is ready to start the final offensive against Black's King.

19...Qe7?

20.g4 c4

21.g5! Nd7 (136)

So far White has shown amazing restraint, but now he lashes out with all his strength.

22.Qxh6!!

This splendid move forces the opening of the g-file and allows White's Rooks to participate in the attack.

22...gxh6

23.gxh6+ Kf8

24.Rg8+!

Black resigns rather than meet his fate. Otherwise, after capturing the Rook, White's h-pawn would advance with tempo, promote to a Queen, and checkmate at the same time with 24...Kxg8 25.h7+ Kf8 26.h8=Q Checkmate.

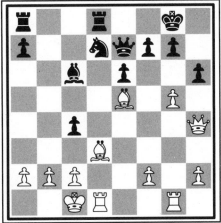

DIAGRAM 136.

Other Plays

The position in Diagram 137 has a more modern look than that of the games of Adolf Anderssen and Paul Morphy because both sides have developed their respective armies. The dark squares around Black's King are weak because Black is missing his Bishop on the a1–h8 diagonal. White takes

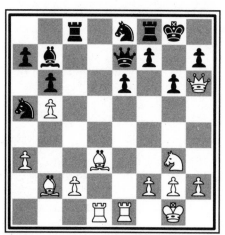

DIAGRAM 137. White to play.
Spielmann–Honlinger
Vienna, 1929

advantage of this weakness with a series of powerful blows: **1.Nf5!!** **Qc5** (the Knight is taboo because 1...gxf5 2.Bxf5 f6 3.Bxe6+ Kh8 4.Bxc8 earns White a decisive material edge) **2.Re5!** (the Rook joins in the attack with tempo) **2...Bd5** **3.Ne7+!!** (a beautiful clearance sacrifice that allows the White Rook to move laterally). Black resigns rather than face 3...Qxe7 4.Qxh7+! Kxh7 5.Rh5+ (which reveals the point of 2.Re5 and 3.Ne7+—the Rook cannot be captured because the g6-pawn is pinned) 5...Kg8 6.Rh8 Checkmate.

CHAPTER SEVENTEEN

Frank Marshall

(1877–1944)

Born in New York, Frank Marshall was US Champion from 1909 to 1935. Like Rudolf Spielmann, Marshall was a throwback to a previous chess era, and he quickly became known as a very tricky player who often swindled his way to victory. Reuben Fine claimed that he had met no one, not even Alexander Alekhine, who had a keener eye for the purely tactical and combinative side of chess.

In spite of his keen eye, poor Marshall usually got stomped when he played extended matches against such giants as Emanuel Lasker (in 1907) and José Raúl Capablanca (in 1909). They simply avoided his tricks. By playing for strategically difficult positions—in Lasker's case—or for simple positions—in Capablanca's case—they created situations in which Marshall's tactical and combinative strengths failed to make an impression.

The Lasker and Capablanca matches represented new developments in chess strategy. The Lasker contest was an example of strategic confusion, whereas the Capablanca contest was a battle of extremely different styles: Capablanca's "simplicity first" style vs. Marshall's crazed "bombs away" style. Marshall was unable to develop effective plans for dealing with either opponent, and he never knew what hit him!

Though Marshall didn't do well against the chess gods, he nevertheless had his moments in the sun, dismantling most of the other masters in decisive fashion.

The Pipe Game
Marshall–A. Burn
Paris, 1900

Britisher Amos Burn loved to smoke a pipe while looking over the possibilities on the board. In "The Pipe Game," Marshall beat Burn so quickly that Burn was never able to get his blasted pipe lit!

1.d4 d5

2.c4 e6

3.Nc3 Nf6

4.Bg5 Be7

5.e3 0-0

Black's defense, known as the Queen's Gambit Declined, is as old as the hills and is a solid and sturdy choice.

6.Nf3 b6

7.Bd3 Bb7

8.cxd5 exd5

So far, the players have calmly played the Queen's Gambit Declined. Now White introduces some risk into the position.

9.Bxf6 Bxf6

10.h4

White makes it clear that he intends to sacrifice a piece with 11.Bxh7+ Kxh7 12.Ng5+, and Black promptly goes out of his way to prevent the sacrifice. (Theoreticians realized 50 years later that the sacrifice beginning with 11.Bxh7+ is not sound in this position.)

10...g6

Black stops White's threat but allows h5 and the subsequent opening of the h-file. When Marshall wanted to attack, it was no easy matter to stop him!

11.h5 Re8

12.hxg6 hxg6

13.Qc2 (138)

At this point, Black thinks his position is quite safe. Burn is reaching for a match to start his pipe when Marshall shocks him with a piece sacrifice.

13...Bg7

14.Bxg6! fxg6

The forgotten match goes out in Burn's fingers.

15.Qxg6 Nd7

16.Ng5

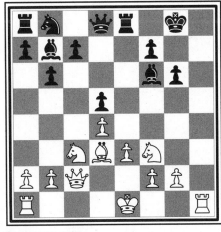

DIAGRAM 138.

White threatens 17.Qf7 Checkmate.

16...Qf6

The expected 17.Qh7+ Kf8 will allow Black's King to run to safety.

17.Rh8+!

Black resigns. Marshall's last move struck like a thunderbolt. Because the Black Bishop is pinned and can't take the White Rook, the Black King is forced to make the capture and move into the corner. Then 17...Kxh8 18.Qh7 is checkmate.

A scintillating example of Marshall's attacking style! When it worked, it worked well. And it seemed to work better in tournaments than in matches. Marshall greatly preferred the variety of opponents found in tournaments to facing the same, well-prepared foe game after game. He said that he wanted "novelties in opening play, slashing attack and counterattack. The grim business of wearing down your opponent has never appealed to me very much."

Marshall–A. Rubinstein
Lodz, 1908

Here's another game that is typical of Marshall. Always happy to take chances, Marshall's gamble pays off when, with both Kings under heavy fire, his renowned opponent gets confused.

1.d4 d5

2.c4 e6

3.Nc3 c5

4.cxd5 exd5

5.Nf3 Nf6?!

The opening is the Tarrasch Defense. Black's fifth move is now known to be a mistake because it allows White to pin. The correct move is 5...Nc6, when a struggle lies ahead.

6.Bg5 Be7

7.dxc5 Be6

8.Rc1 0-0

9.Bxf6

White pulls Black's Bishop away from the c5-pawn. Later, analysts decided that 9.e3 is the best move because it gives White a superior position.

9...Bxf6

10.e3 Qa5

11.a3 Nc6

12.Bd3 Qxc5

Black regains his pawn, and the game is roughly balanced. The isolation of Black's d-pawn is compensated by his powerful dark-squared Bishop.

A modern master would now move his King to safety with 13.0-0, but Marshall had no patience for safety-first measures. As a chess player, he lived for the attack!

13.h4?

Such wing attacks are usually successful only if you control the center or if the center is closed. Here, the center is open and can be changed by Black (d5–d4), so White's Kingside action is suspicious and seems destined to fail.

13...Qe7

14.Ng5 h6

15.Nxe6 fxe6

16.Bb1

White intends to play Qd3 followed by Qh7+, harassing Black's monarch. All very promising.

16...Bxh4!

Black starts his counterattack by battering White's f-pawn with both his Bishop and Rook.

17.g3 Bxg3!

The destruction of the pawns that shielded White's King leaves the White monarch in great peril.

18.fxg3 Qg5

19.Qd3

Both sides are swinging for the fences. With this move, White defends the e-pawn and prepares for Qh7+, hoping to kick-start his own attack.

19...Qxg3+?

A tempting but incorrect move. Black should play 19...Ne5!, which leads to 20.Qh7+ Kf7 21.Rf1+ Ke7, when his King has run to safety but White's is still on the firing line.

20.Kd2 Rf2+

21.Ne2 Ne5

22.Qh7+ Kf7

23.Rc7+ Kf6 (139)

Black thinks he is doing well in the position shown in Diagram 139, but he has overlooked the possibility of White's next shot.

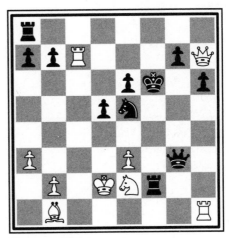

DIAGRAM 139.

24.Rxh6+!

Black resigns. Marshall's last move was a clearance sacrifice. By forcing Rubinstein to capture the Rook, he moved the g7-pawn aside, and the e7-square became available to his Queen. Rubinstein resigned because 24...gxh6 25.Qe7 Checkmate is unstoppable.

Other Plays

Marshall was always a favorite with the crowds, and it's not hard to understand why. Take, for example, the following position, from which he made a move that stunned the chess world and became known as one of the most brilliant moves ever played! As you can see in Diagram 140, Black is ahead a piece, but White is attacking both Black's Queen and his h3-Rook. Black's move is a beauty: **1...Qg3!!**. He invites White to capture his Queen in any of three ways. White resigns! Why? It turns out that all three captures lead to White's defeat. Let's look at each one:

DIAGRAM 140.   Black to play.
Lewitzky–Marshall
Breslau, 1912

- 2.fxg3 Ne2+ 3.Kh1 Rxf1, with a back rank checkmate.

- 2.hxg3 Ne2 Checkmate.

- 2.Qxg3 Ne2+ 3.Kh1 Nxg3+ 4.Kg1 (a forced move because both the h- and f-pawns are pinned) 4...Nxf1, which leads to an easy win in the ending for Black.

CHAPTER EIGHTEEN

Alexander Alekhine

(1892–1946)

Born in Moscow to a wealthy family, Alexander Alekhine has the morbid distinction of being the only man to die while holding the World Champion title. A player of extraordinary tactical vision, Alekhine was also the first great theorist of openings. Pushed by a burning ambition to win the World Championship, Alekhine realized that tactical ability alone was not enough to take him to the peak. By tireless study, Alekhine mastered all phases of the game. He is in many respects the prototype of the modern Grandmaster. By thoroughly studying openings and intensely analyzing his opponent's games, Alekhine broke a new trail to greatness that has been followed by many of today's professional chess players.

Not a very likeable man, Alekhine was a drunk and a Nazi sympathizer. Nevertheless, he achieved such a high playing level that many chess fans rank him with Capablanca, Lasker, Fischer, and Kasparov as one of the five greatest players who ever lived.

Alekhine–O. Chajes
Carlsbad, 1911

Let's look at a game that has the Alekhine stamp all over it. A sharp opening is followed by forceful play that culminates in a crisp tactical finish. Note particularly Alekhine's tactical mastery, which he uses to gain material and achieve eventual victory.

1.c4

This is the English Opening, which was rarely seen in those days. Alekhine liked to play a variety of openings, many of which were ahead of his time.

1...e6

2.e4 c5

3.Nc3 Nc6

4.Nf3 g6

Not a good choice. Black will now be left with dark-square holes, particularly the d6-square, resembling swiss cheese.

5.d4 cxd4

6.Nxd4 Bg7

7.Ndb5!

White is already threatening to play Nd6 and jump in with check. Black is in trouble, and the opening has barely begun! (This game shows why a careful study of openings is mandatory. Alekhine made his contemporaries, who lacked an understanding of openings, look like beginners.)

7...Be5

8.f4 a6

9.fxe5 axb5

10.Bf4

By defending his e5-pawn, White keeps up the pressure on the d6- and f6-squares.

10...bxc4

11.Bxc4

Black's game is horrible. In addition to the holes that riddle his position, he is behind in development and threatened with Nb5–d6.

11...Ra5

A little trap. Black is hoping for 12.Nb5? Rxb5 13.Bxb5 Qa5+ followed by 14...Qxb5, which would win him two pieces for a Rook.

12.0-0!

Alekhine moves his King to safety and places his Rook on the half-open f-file.

12...b5

Black is still trying to tempt 13.Nxb5? Rxb5 14.Bxb5 Qb6+ followed by 15...Qxb5, for a gain of material. He avoids 12...Nxe5 13.Bxe5 Rxe5 because 14.Qd6! followed by 15.Nb5 would be crushing.

13.b4!! (141)

Fabulous! Black's next moves are somewhat forced because a Rook retreat would permit White to capture the b5-pawn at his leisure. In his game notes, Alekhine calculated that an upcoming pin would lead to Chajes's destruction.

13...Qb6+

14.Kh1 Nxb4

Black must go along with White's agenda to avoid 14...Ra8 15.Nxb5.

15.Bxb5 Rxb5

16.Nxb5 Qxb5

17.Rb1!

This is the position Alekhine foresaw when he played 13.b4. The pin is decisive. Black has four possible

DIAGRAM 141.

responses, of which he rejects these three:

- 17...Qc5 18.Rc1, which skewers the Queen and Bishop.
- 17...Qc4 18.Qa4, which creates a pin on the 4th rank and loses the Black Knight.
- 17...Qa5 18.Bd2—yet another pin—which also loses the Black Knight.

In desperation, Black tries the fourth alternative.

17...Ba6

18.Qd6 f6

19.Rfc1

The Knight is not going away. The immediate 19.Qxb4?? Qxb4 20.Rxb4 would allow ...Bxf1, clipping a Rook.

19...Qd3

20.Rxb4

White now has an extra Exchange and can attack Black's King. The final moves are not of great interest.

20...g5

21.Rd4 Qb5

22.a4 Qb7

23.Rc7 Qb1+

24.Rd1

Black resigns.

R. Réti–Alekhine
Baden-Baden, 1925

In 1927, Alekhine challenged José Raúl Capablanca for the World Championship, eventually winning the title in one of the most difficult matches ever played. While preparing for the Championship match, Alekhine played the following game, exhibiting perhaps his most celebrated combination—its depth is truly awesome.

Richard Réti, Alekhine's opponent in this game, was a chess rebel who preached a bunch of new ideas that were labeled "hypermodern." One of the main tenets of hypermodernism concerned the center. The classical old guard preached that success depended on ownership of the center, whereas the hypermoderns insisted that you could allow your opponent to build a big pawn center as long as you could later attack the center from the flanks. Réti began the game like this:

1.g3

The ideas of the hypermoderns were certainly not lost on Alekhine. He took the best ideas from each school of chess thought and mixed them together to come up with a system of his own.

1...e5

2.Nf3!?

White's move is a little risky because his Knight gets pushed around with loss of tempo. However, he is willing to run hither and thither with this Knight, hoping to goad Black's pawns forward so that he can later attack them. He wants to show that they are not strong, but merely targets.

Compare the ideas of Réti with those of players from Anderssen's and Morphy's era, and you will be struck by the vast difference in their thinking. The time of chess professionalism, and the strategic thought that comes with it, had arrived.

The game continues:

2...e4

3.Nd4 d5

4.d3 exd3

5.Qxd3?!

This early Queen development is too provocative. A better move is 5.cxd3, which brings a flank pawn into the center.

5...Nf6

6.Bg2 Bb4+

7.Bd2 Bxd2+

8.Nxd2 0-0

Black has moved his King to safety and is ready to make use of the half-open e-file. Next, he must find good squares for his Queenside pieces.

9.c4 Na6

10.cxd5 Nb4

11.Qc4 Nbxd5

12.N2b3 c6

13.0-0 Re8

14.Rfd1 Bg4!

15.Rd2 Qc8

16.Nc5

White has played well and has found excellent squares for his Knights. He plans an attack on the Queenside with b2–b4–b5.

16...Bh3!

Black starts a counterattack on the Kingside, setting a nasty trap.

Keep in mind that you should never set a trap without expecting your opponent to see the threat. If he misses it, you can congratulate yourself on your nice win. If he sees it, your move should nevertheless improve your position in some way. In this case, Réti sees through the trap.

17.Bf3

The greedy 17.Bxh3? leads to 17...Qxh3 18.Nxb7 Ng4 19.Nf3 Nde3! 20.fxe3 Nxe3 (threatening 21...Qg2 Checkmate) 21.Qxf7+! Kh8! (not 21...Kxf7 22.Ng5+, forking Black's King and Queen) 22.Nh4 Rf8 and an eventual Black win, because if the Queen moves, then 23...Rf1+ leads to checkmate.

This cunningly laid trap was typical of Alekhine's imaginative play. Only the finest players could avoid failure in the face of such tactics. But unlike players of several decades earlier, Réti had no compunctions about refusing a material offer and side-stepping the trap.

17...Bg4

18.Bg2 Bh3

19.Bf3 Bg4

20.Bh1

White bravely plays for a win, avoiding 20.Bg2, which leads to a three time repetition and a draw.

20...h5!

Black has set up the conditions he needs for a successful Kingside offensive. White's pieces have made headway on the Queenside, but they have wandered far from White's King, and White's h1-Bishop is on a poor defensive square. Even so, White's pawns provide good cover for his King. Black intends to use his h-pawn to open White's Kingside pawn shield.

21.b4 a6

22.Rc1 h4

23.a4 hxg3

24.hxg3 Qc7

Black has targeted the g3-pawn as the weak point, so he aims his Queen at it and prepares to mow it down.

25.b5 axb5

26.axb5 (142)

Both players have pursued their plans, and Diagram 142 shows an innocent-enough setting. White has made substantial gains on the Queenside, and Black has been working on the Kingside. Black now unleashes a combination of incredible depth. Combinations like this one led Bobby Fischer to call Alekhine "the deepest player that ever lived."

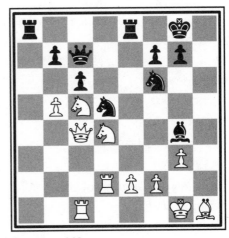

DIAGRAM 142.

26...Re3!!

Black trains his guns on the weakened g3-pawn. Now 27.fxe3?? Qxg3+ 28.Bg2 Bh3 leads to checkmate and 27.bxc6 Rxg3+! is also horrible. White has to pull back his pieces from the Queenside to protect his monarch.

27.Nf3

The best defense was 27.Bf3! Bxf3 28.exf3 (though Reuben Fine maintains that after 28...cxb5 29.Nxb5 Qa5, Black would retain the advantage).

27...cxb5

28.Qxb5 Nc3!

Black forks the White Queen and e2-pawn.

29.Qxb7 Qxb7

30.Nxb7 Nxe2+

31.Kh2

This move is better for White than 31.Kf1, which would lead to Nxg3+ 32.fxg3 Bxf3 33.Bxf3 Rxf3+ and the loss of a pawn. After 31.Kh2, White thinks the worst is over, but Black has more in store. He realizes that White's far-flung b7-Knight lacks protection.

31...Ne4!

Now 32.fxe3 Nxd2 means Black will win the Exchange. However, the real point of 31...Ne4 becomes apparent only with the 42nd move!

32.Rc4!

White hopes for 32...Nxd2 33.Nxd2! or 32...Bxf3 33.Rxe4!, with good chances of a draw.

32...Nxf2

33.Bg2 Be6!

34.Rc2 Ng4+

35.Kh3

Not exactly the type of move White wants to play, but 35.Kh1 Ra1+ is a winning check!

35...Ne5+

36.Kh2 Rxf3!

37.Rxe2 Ng4+

38.Kh3 Ne3+

39.Kh2 Nxc2

40.Bxf3 Nd4

Black forks the White Rook and Bishop and White resigns rather than play 41.Re3 Nxf3+ 42.Rxf3. Bd5!, when the new fork by the Black Bishop leads to the capture of the White Knight.

An amazing game, and a far cry from the little combinations we are used to seeing from lesser mortals! Such tremendous tactical vision is extremely rare. If you soared like I did when, as a 14-year-old, I saw it for the first time, then recounting this great game has been a pleasure for us both. Like a beautiful painting, I have presented this work of art as something to marvel at and enjoy. If this book has helped you unlock the secrets of this combination and appreciate it just a little, then I am well pleased.

Alekhine–Em. Lasker
Zürich, 1934

The last Alekhine gem I'll cover shows him destroying the immortal Emanuel Lasker.

1.d4 d5

2.c4 e6

3.Nc3 Nf6

4.Nf3 Be7

5.Bg5 Nbd7

6.e3 0-0

7.Rc1 c6

8.Bd3 dxc4

9.Bxc4 Nd5

Black's ninth move was introduced by José Raúl Capablanca as a maneuver to free up space in the Queen's Gambit Declined. Black is following the strategic principle that the side with less territory should exchange some pieces to relieve the cramp.

10.Bxe7 Qxe7

11.Ne4

This is Alekhine's invention. The mature Alekhine is quite happy to go directly into 11...Qb4+ 12.Qd2 Qxd2+ 13.Kxd2, with a slightly superior endgame.

11...N5f6

12.Ng3 e5

13.0-0 exd4

14.Nf5

A better move is probably 14.exd4 followed by 15.Re1, when White introduces his Rook with tempo. Eventually Black would obtain equality.

14...Qd8

15.N3xd4 Ne5

16.Bb3 Bxf5

17.Nxf5 Qb6?

This move is the cause of Black's future problems. The forcing 17...g6 would chase the f5-Knight away from its fine position and equalize the game.

The position seemed rather simple a move or two ago, but now Alekhine takes the initiative and, creating threat after threat, never lets up.

18.Qd6! Ned7

19.Rfd1 Rad8

20.Qg3 g6

21.Qg5!

Now, Rd6 threatens to hit Black's Knight.

21...Kh8

22.Nd6

And here, 23.Nxf7+ threatens to munch material.

22...Kg7

23.e4!

The e-pawn joins in the attack. This move also frees the 3rd rank for White's Rooks to come to the Kingside.

23...Ng8

24.Rd3

White correctly brings in reinforcements to get to Black's King.

24...f6

As you can see in Diagram 143, a pretty pattern would result from 24...h6 25.Nf5+ Kh7 26.Nxh6! f6 27.Nf5! fxg5 28.Rh3+ with checkmate to follow.

25.Nf5+ Kh8

26.Qxg6!

Black resigns. Lasker laid down his King because he had no desire to suffer through 26...hxg6 27.Rh3+ Nh6 28.Rxh6 Checkmate. A devastating victory for Alekhine.

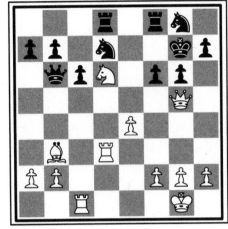

DIAGRAM 143.

CHAPTER NINETEEN

Mikhail Tal

(1936–1992)

When Alexander Alekhine died in 1946, there were no tactical wizards waiting in the wings to take his place. The science of pure chess took center stage, and the chief of the scientists, Mikhail Botvinnik, reigned from 1948 to 1960, with the exception of a one-year period when he lost the title to Vasily Smyslov—winning it back in a rematch. This impressive performance seemed to indicate that all future World Champions would be positional players. Little did the chess world suspect that another firebrand would appear and take the game by storm.

Mikhail Tal was born in Riga, Latvia, in 1936. During his professional career, his style was characterized by risk and daring, and he reveled in tactical duels and complex combinations. A man of unbelievable tactical vision, he was able to calculate long, complicated variations after merely glancing at a position. Considered to be an unsound player, he nevertheless confounded his critics by consistently winning tournament after tournament. In 1960, at the tender age of 24, Tal achieved the unthinkable,

175

knocking Botvinnik aside and claiming the World Champion title as his own. Botvinnik said:

> I was surprised by his ability to figure out complex variations. Then the way he sets out the game; he was not interested in the objectivity of the position, whether it's better or worse, he only needed room for his pieces. All you do then is figure out variations which are extremely difficult. He was tactically outplaying me and I made mistakes.

Did Tal's coronation mean that a new era of attacking play was at hand? Many players thought so, and some coaches went so far as to insist that their students play aggressively and sacrifice whenever possible. As Tal put it:

> These poor young players must have breathed a sigh of relief when I lost the title back to Botvinnik (in 1961). Now they could play calm positional chess again!

As we go to press with this book, we are stunned to learn of the death of Mikhail Tal at the age of 55. We are all the poorer for his loss. His games will be his everlasting memorial.

Tal–Miller
Simultaneous
Los Angeles, 1988

The first Tal game we'll look at is remarkable not because Tal was playing a simultaneous exhibition of 20 to 40 games (most top players can handle this type of simultaneous exhibition), but because he defeated his opponent in such a stunning way. Instead of being upset at his loss, Tal's victim wore a beaming smile after the game. After all, by losing to a piece of typical Tal brilliance, he became part of the Tal legend. Here's the game:

1.e4 e5

2.Nf3 Nc6

3.Bc4 Nf6

By playing the complicated Two Knights' Defense, Black indicates his desire to beat his illustrious opponent.

4.d4

White strives for the initiative, rejecting the critical 4.Ng5 d5 5.exd5 Na5 6.Bb5+ c6 7.dxc6 bxc6, which gives Black the initiative as compensation for his sacrificed pawn.

4...d6

A bit passive. The best move is 4....exd4, with equal chances.

5.dxe5 Nxe4

6.Bxf7+

A tiny combination. White gets his piece back right away.

6...Kxf7

7.Qd5+

White forks the Black King and e4-Knight.

7...Be6

8.Qxe4

The smoke clears to reveal that White's combination has produced dramatic results. He is up a pawn, and Black's King is uncomfortably placed on f7.

8...Be7

9.0-0 d5

10.Qd3 Qd7

11.Re1 Raf8

12.Nc3 Ke8

13.Ng5 Bc5

14.Nxe6!?

Now White moves into a realm of great complexity.

14...Bxf2+

15.Kh1 Bxe1

16.Nxf8 Rxf8

17.Bg5

White's move threatens 18.Rxe1 and capture of the Black Bishop. However, Black notices that he can create a back rank checkmate with ...Rf1 if he can force White's Queen away from the defense of the f1-square.

17...Nb4

18.Qe2 Nxc2!

This chance to battle Tal tactically on a one-to-one basis must have given Black great pleasure. Now 19.Qxc2 is not possible because 19....Rf1 results in checkmate.

19.e6 Qd6

20.Nb5! Qe5!

At this point, the spectators thought that Black would win. White's Queen, Rook, and Bishop all hang because 21.Qxe5?? loses to 21...Rf1 Checkmate. How can White survive?

21.h4!! (144)

Simply superb. White's move defends his Bishop, stops the back rank checkmate, and threatens to capture Black's Queen. And as if that weren't enough, 21...Qxe2 and 21....Qxb2 both run into 22.Nxc7 Checkmate. "So we were wrong," cried the audience, "Tal was winning all along."

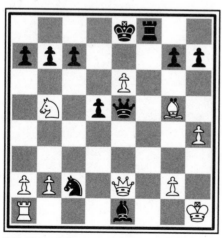

DIAGRAM 144.

21...Qg3!

Black threatens both ...Nxa1 and ...Rf2. Excitement mounts in the crowd! Will Black win after all?

22.Rd1!!

The tricky point of White's play! Now 22...c6 is strongly countered by 23.Rd3! Qb8 24.Rf3!, when 24...cxb5 loses to 25.Qxb5+. However, Black has another option.

22...Rf2

White must now find some way to answer Black's threat of ...Qxg2 Checkmate.

23.Qxf2!!

Now White's intentions are finally clear.

23...Bxf2

Black's alternative 23...Qxf2 24.Nxc7+ Kf8 25.e7+ Kg8 26.e8=Q+, is an easy win for White.

24.Rxd5

The threat of 25.Rd8 Checkmate forces Black to part with material. (Notice how Tal has fashioned a checkmating net with his Rook, Bishop, and pawn.)

24...Qxh4+

25.Bxh4 Bxh4

26.Nxc7+

White, a full Exchange up, can win as he pleases.

26...Kf8

27.Rf5+ Bf6

28.Rd5 a6

29.Rd7 Nb4

30.Rf7+ Kg8

31.Rxf6!

Another tactic. After 31...gxf6 32.e7, the pawn will become a Queen.

31...Nc6

32.Rf7 g6

33.e7!

Black resigns.

Tal–Forbis
Simultaneous
Chicago, 1988

The next game was also played in a simultaneous exhibition, so once again, keep in mind that these brilliant moves occurred while Tal was playing more than 30 games at once!

1.e4 c5

2.Nf3 d6

3.d4 cxd4

4.Nxd4 Nf6

5.Nc3 g6

6.Be3 Bg7

7.f3 Nc6

8.Qd2 0-0

9.Bc4

This is the Dragon Variation of the Sicilian. The Dragon leads to violent struggles and suits the desires of both players.

9...Nd7!?

Black has enjoyed excellent results in other games with this rare sideline, so he decides to use it here.

10.h4 Nb6

11.Bb3 Na5

12.h5 Nbc4

13.Qe2 Nxe3

14.Qxe3 Nxb3

15.axb3 Bd7

Black has managed to eat both of White's attacking Bishops. Does the fact that his opponent lost time while executing this maneuver compensate White enough for the capture of his clerics?

16.0-0-0 e6

17.f4! Qb6

18.f5!

White tries to crack open the enemy King's defenses before Black's Bishops can do any damage.

18...gxf5

The greedy alternative, 18...e5, loses to 19.Nd5 exd4 20.Ne7+ Kh8 21.hxg6 fxg6 22.fxg6 dxe3 23.Rxh7 Checkmate.

19.exf5 Kh8

20.Rhf1 Bxd4?

A calmer reaction is 20...Rg8, when 21.f6 can be met by 21...Bf8 with a sharp struggle ahead. However, afraid that his Bishop might be buried, Black quickly exchanges it.

21.Rxd4 e5

Black hopes after 22..Rd3 Qxe3+ to trade Queens. White, of course, has no intention of exchanging his most powerful attack weapon.

22.Qh6!

White offers up his Rook.

22...Qxd4

23.Qf6+ Kg8

24.Nd5!! (145)

The alternative 24.Qg5+ Kh8 25.h6 would be met by 25...e4 and result in the Black Queen's defense of the g7-square. Also useless is 24.h6 Qg4, with the Queen once again defending the g7-square. After 24.Nd5, Black can't capture the Knight with 24...Qxd5 because 25.Qg5+ Kh8 26.h6 Rg8 27.Qf6+ leads to checkmate.

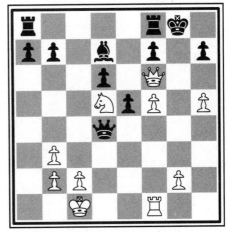

White's brilliant 24th move is a deflection sacrifice. He offers his Knight so that Black's Queen will be drawn away from the a1–h8 diagonal. Then Black no longer has the possibility of ...e4 because his Queen is no longer defending the g7-square.

24...Rfe8

Black stops the threatened 25.Ne7 Checkmate.

25.Qg5+ Kh8

26.h6

DIAGRAM 145.

Another threat: 27.Qg7 Checkmate.

    26...e4

    27.f6

White blocks Black's Queen and once again threatens Qg7 Checkmate.

    27...Rg8

    28.Qg7+! Rxg7

    29.hxg7+ Kg8

    30.Ne7 Checkmate!

Absolutely amazing!

Gurgenidze–Tal
Moscow, 1957

This chapter's final game shows how the young Tal played against other Grandmasters. He often destroyed them as easily as he destroyed the amateurs in the previous games!

    1.d4 Nf6

    2.c4 c5

    3.d5 e6

Black's use of this Modern Benoni System completely revitalized the whole opening.

    4.Nc3 exd5

    5.cxd5 d6

    6.Nf3 g6

    7.e4 Bg7

    8.Be2 0-0

    9.0-0 Re8

The pressure is on White's e4-pawn. Usually Black tries to use his Queen-side pawn majority by playing for a ...b7–b5 advance, and White tries to use his central pawn majority by playing for an e4–e5 advance. In this game, none of these strategies materializes because White's King ends up on the firing line!

10.Nd2 Na6

11.Re1 Nc7

This Knight was placed here to help Black play for ...b7–b5.

12.a4

That's the end of Black's threatened Queenside expansion.

12...b6

13.Qc2 Ng4

The threat of 14...Qh4 seems to force White to play 14.Bxg4 with chances for both players. Instead, White innocently tries to chase the Knight back.

14.h3? Nxf2!! (146)

As you can see in Diagram 146, all thoughts of subtle pawn majority play dissolve as Black sacrifices a Knight and starts a King hunt.

15.Kxf2 Qh4+

16.Kf1

Playing 16.Kg1 is impossible because of 16...Qxe1+, and 16.g3 Bd4+ forces checkmate.

16...Bd4

17.Nd1

White covers the checkmate on f2. With 18.Nf3 to come, he thinks he is safe, but Black's next move comes as a rude shock.

17...Qxh3!

Black bursts through White's King-side and threatens 18...Qh1 with checkmate. Note that 18.gxh3?? is bad because the pretty 18...Bxh3 is checkmate.

18.Bf3 Qh2

19.Ne3 f5!

Black calmly plays to open new lines of attack.

DIAGRAM 146.

20.Ndc4 fxe4

21.Bxe4 Ba6

White's Knight is pinned, and Black threatens 22...Bxc4+ 23.Nxc4 (or 23.Qxc4 Rxe4) 23...Qg1 24.Ke2 Qxg2+, with an easy win.

22.Bf3 Re5

Black is preparing to double his Rooks on the e-file. White is powerless to stop him from building up for the final assault.

23.Ra3 Rae8

24.Bd2 Nxd5!

Now every Black piece is taking part in the battle.

25.Bxd5+

White avoids 25.Nxd5?? Qg1 Checkmate.

25...Rxd5

26.Ke2

Playing 26.Nxd5 loses to 26...Qg1 Checkmate. With 26.Ke2, White hopes to run his King to the safety of the Queenside, but he is shot down.

26...Bxe3

27.Rxe3 Bxc4+

White resigns because neither 28.Qxc4 Qxg2+ 29.Kd1 Qxd2 Checkmate nor 28.Kd1 Rxe3 29.Rxe3 Qxg2 are very attractive.

It doesn't take a genius to figure out why Tal was the public's favorite chess player for a long, long time!

CHAPTER TWENTY

Garry Kasparov

(1963–)

After Mikhail Botvinnik regained his title in 1961, players with positional styles once again held the highest chess titles. The world of chess was dominated by the likes of Tigran Petrosyan, with his motto of "safety first"; Boris Spassky, who had an aggressive, universal style; and Bobby Fischer, who had a very clear, simple, classic style. In 1975, Anatoly Karpov won the title by default from Fischer.

Thereafter, Karpov set out to prove that he deserved to be World Champion. With his refined, dry style and relentless precision, he crushed everyone in sight. People dreamed of a Tal-like player who would rise up and brighten the chess world with tactical fantasy.

The dream became reality when Garry Kasparov won the title from Karpov in 1985 at just 22 years of age! Born in Baku, Azerbaijan, Kasparov is considered by many to be a reincarnation of Alexander Alekhine. A master of all openings, Kasparov slices and dices his opponents with a combinative vision that is every bit the equal of Tal's and Alekhine's. The excitement of Kasparov's style has revitalized interest in chess.

In the following three contests, we'll see how Kasparov crushes his opponents. All three opponents are among the world's strongest Grandmasters, but none of them can stand up to Kasparov's hammer-like blows.

Hübner–Kasparov
Hamburg, 1985
Match Game 1

In a six-game training match, Kasparov clobbered Germany's top player. The match ended in a 4½-to-1½ victory for Kasparov. This, the first game of the match, was an indication of things to come.

1.c4

The English Opening. A couple of years after this game, Kasparov started playing this opening himself.

1...e5

2.Nc3 d6

3.d4 exd4

4.Qxd4 Nf6

5.g3 Nc6

6.Qd2

This move seems to block the dark-squared Bishop, but White actually intends to develop this Bishop on the a1-h8 diagonal with b3 and Bb2.

6...Be6

7.Nd5 Ne5

8.b3 Ne4

9.Qe3 Nc5!?

10.Bb2?

This natural move turns out badly because after ...c6 and ...Qa5 it exposes White to check along the a5–e1 diagonal. Correct is 10.Bg2! c6 11.Nc3 a5, with opportunities for both players.

10...c6

11.Nf4?

Another poor move. Imperative is 11.Nc3 Ng4 12.Qd4 Be7, which keeps Black's advantage to a minimum. Now White is put on the defensive, and he never recovers.

11...Ng4!

12.Qd4?!

Confused, White allows himself to be dragged into a tactical grinder. A better move is 12.Nxe6 Nxe3 13.Nxd8 Nc2+ 14.Kd1 Nxa1 15.Nxf7 Kxf7 16.Bxa1 Bxe7, even though Black then has a big advantage.

12...Ne4!! (147)

A shocker that hangs the Black Knight in midair. As you can see in Diagram 147, the immediate threats are 13...Ngxf2 and 13...Qa5+. White faces disaster after only twelve moves.

13.Bh3

White's King now has f1 to run to. White avoids 13.Qxe4 Qa5+ 14.Kd1 Nxf2+, which produces a royal fork. Also unpleasant is 13.Ngh3 Qa5+ 14.Kd1 d5, with a crushing attack. (You don't want your King running around in the center against Kasparov!)

13...Qa5!+

Black doesn't fall for 13...Ngxf2? 14.Bxe6 fxe6 15.Nxe6 Qa5+ 16.Bc3!, which leaves matters far from clear.

14.Kf1 Ngxf2

15.Bxe6

After 15.Nxe6 fxe6 16.Bxe6 Be7! 17.Qxg7 Rf8 18.Kg2 Nxh1 19.Kxh1 Qd2, Black still has a winning attack.

15...fxe6

16.Nxe6 Kd7!

This move attacks the White Knight, prepares the way for a Rook on e8,

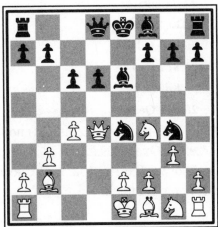

DIAGRAM 147.

187

and stops any future Knight forks that White might make with Nc7. One of the keys to good chess is making moves that further both defensive and attacking plans at the same time.

17.Nh3 Nxh3!

18.Qxe4 Re8

19.Nc5+

Desperate, White is trying to draw the Black Queen away from the d2-square. If he plays 19.Qg4 instead, Rxe6 20.Qxh3 Qd2 leads to a crushing double attack against b2 and e2.

19...Qxc5

20.Qg4+ Kc7

21.Qxh3 Be7!

Black's remaining forces quietly join in the attack. The great attackers always seem to know when to pause and bring up reinforcements. Of course, Black cares nothing for the g7-pawn.

22.Bxg7 Rhf8+!

This Exchange sacrifice initiates the final phase of the game—a direct attack on the White King.

23.Bxf8 Rxf8+

24.Ke1 Qf2+

25.Kd1 Qd4+

26.Kc2 Qe4+!

27.Kd2 Bg5+

28.Kc3 Qe5+

White resigns—he has suffered enough. The finish would have been 29.Kb4 (or 29.Kc2 Qxe2+) 29...Bd2+ 30.Ka3 Bc3 31.Qxh7+ Kb8, after which the dual threat of 32...Bxa1 and 32...Qa5 Checkmate leads to White's demise. A typical Kasparov attack.

Kasparov–U. Andersson
Tilburg, 1981

Because of his style of play, Ulf Andersson is considered to be one of the world's most difficult players to beat. Whereas many players seek action and attacking chances for their own pieces, Andersson's goal is simply to stymie the activity of his opponent's pieces. The would-be attacker becomes increasingly frustrated, often lashing out with an unsound sacrifice that this defense-minded Grandmaster simply pockets. However, as you'll see in this game, the 18-year-old Kasparov did not seem to be impressed!

1.d4 Nf6

2.c4 e6

3.Nf3 b6

4.a3

This is the Petrosyan System of the Queen's Indian Defense, which is one of Kasparov's most potent weapons.

4...Bb7

5.Nc3 Ne4

The more common 5...d5 leads to a harder struggle. (Because Kasparov is a renowned expert in this type of play, Andersson wants to keep things quiet and therefore provokes an exchange of pieces.)

6.Nxe4 Bxe4

7.Nd2! Bg6?!

The retreat 7...Bb7 is better.

8.g3!

Now White's Bishop can take control of the long diagonal.

8...Nc6

9.e3 a6?

This passive move wastes time and allows White to gain some territory on the Queenside.

10.b4! b5

11.cxb5 axb5

12.Bb2

White avoids 12.Bxb5? Nxb4! because the pin along the a-file prevents him from capturing the Black Knight.

12...Na7

Black is forced to move his Knight to this terrible square because the b-pawn is in need of defense.

13.h4!

Suddenly, White lashes out on the Kingside. This space-gaining move threatens 14.h5 Bf5 15.g4, which traps the Black Bishop.

13...h6

Black gives his Bishop the h7-square to run to.

14.d5!

This pawn sacrifice gives White's b2-Bishop room for maximum activity. (Kasparov's main concern in chess is not material but rather gain of tempo and the activity potential of his pieces.)

14...exd5

15.Bg2 c6

More gain of tempo. White trades an aggressive piece move (which develops the piece) for Black's defensive pawn move.

16.0-0

Now White is fully mobilized and ready to start a furious attack.

16...f6

Black blocks the a1–h8 diagonal. He would love to play 16...Be7 and 17...0-0, but any move by his dark-squared Bishop allows 17.Bxg7 and loses a pawn. As a result, Black's King can't evacuate the center as soon as he would like.

17.Rfe1!

White is preparing to rip open the center with e3–e4.

17...Be7

Black is finally ready to castle, but White now jumps on him and doesn't give him the chance.

18.Qg4 Kf7

19.h5 Bh7

20.e4 dxe4

21.Bxe4!

DIAGRAM 148.

Black's last few moves have all been forced. Now White wants to trade the light-squared Bishops so that the light squares in Black's camp (the g6-square in particular) will lose their defender.

21...Bxe4

22.Nxe4 Nc8

23.Rad1 Ra7 (148)

Compare White's powerfully placed central pieces with Black's vulnerable King and groveling army. It should come as no surprise that White now finds a decisive combination.

24.Nxf6!

A crushing blow that smashes through Black's defenses.

24...gxf6

Also hopeless is 24...Bxf6 25.Qg6+ Kf8 26.Bxf6 gxf6 27.Re6!, because when the f6-pawn falls, the Black King falls with it. (The alternative 26...Qxf6 27.Re8 is checkmate.) Note that the White Rook cannot be taken because of the pin on the d-file.

25.Qg6+ Kf8

26.Bc1!

Retreating moves tend to be hard to find. This one threatens 27.Bxh6+, getting to Black's King.

26...d5

27.Rd4!

A masterful building move (Kasparov is in no hurry). The more immediate 27.Bxh6+ Rxh6 28.Qxh6+ Kg8 29.Rd4 Bf8 allows Black to put up some resistance.

27...Nd6

28.Rg4

White keeps bringing new pieces to join the attack. Now he threatens 29.Qg7+, which captures Black's h8-Rook.

28...Nf7

This move defends both h8 and h6. Has White made a mistake?

29.Bxh6+!

This move shatters that illusion. Now 29...Nxh6 30.Qg7+ leads to a decisive material gain, and 29...Rxh6 allows 30.Qg8 Checkmate.

29...Ke8

30.Bg7

Black resigns. After 30...Rg8 31.h6 followed by 32.h7, he can't prevent the promotion of the h-pawn.

Kasparov–Gheorghiu
Moscow, 1982

In 1982, the young Garry Kasparov was emerging as one of the strongest Grandmasters in the world. The 1982 Moscow tournament represented his greatest test to date. Playing against a whole galaxy of chess stars, Kasparov earned second prize behind World Champion Anatoly Karpov. The game I discuss here was critical to Kasparov's high standing. He convincingly took apart Romanian Grandmaster Florin Gheorghiu in the best game of the tournament.

1.d4 Nf6

2.c4 e6

3.Nf3 b6

4.Nc3 Bb7

5.a3 d5

6.cxd5 Nxd5

Black plays one of the critical lines of defense against the Petrosyan System of the Queen's Indian Defense. (Is it wise to get into a slugfest with Kasparov in his favorite opening?)

7.Qc2 c5

8.e4 Nxc3

9.bxc3 Be7

10.Bb5+

White tosses in this move for two reasons: first, because Black's Bishop is not as well placed on c6 as on b7; and second, because this move takes the c6-square away from the Black Knight.

10...Bc6

11.Bd3 Nd7

12.0-0 h6

13.Rfd1 Qc7?

Black had to castle. (As I said, it's not wise to leave your King in the center against this guy!)

14.d5!

The pawn is sacrificed to open up the center files, the route to Black's King. (Kasparov is already smelling blood!)

14...exd5

15.exd5 Bxd5

16.Bb5 a6

Black hopes for 17.Bxd7+ Qxd7 18.c4 Be4!, from which he escapes with minor injuries. He also considered 16...Bc6, but after 17.Bf4! Qb7 18.Bxc6 Qxc6 19.Re1, his King would be stuck in the center for a long time.

17.Bf4! (149)

DIAGRAM 149.

A powerful developing move. As you can see in Diagram 149, White temporarily sacrifices a piece in order to draw Black's Queen away from the defense of the d7-Knight.

    17...Qxf4

    18.Bxd7+ Kxd7

    19.Rxd5+ Kc7?

Black makes the unfortunate decision to run in the wrong direction with his King. The Queenside won't be at all safe. The great attackers often benefit from errors induced by their daring play. Fortune favors the brave.

    20.Re1

All the White pieces are in play in the center, whereas Black's forces are flung all over the place and cannot work together.

    20...Bd6

Black did not like 20...Rhe8 because 21.Rde5 produces an unpleasant pin on the e-file.

    21.Rf5

White never lets up. (Notice how every move Kasparov plays is aggressive and full of purpose.) He follows the advice of the Confederate cavalryman Nathan Bedford Forest who said, "When you got 'em runnin', keep 'em runnin'."

    21...Qc4

Black is trying to protect the f7-pawn.

    22.Re4

This move forces Black's Queen to abandon its defense of the f7-pawn.

    22...Qb5

    23.Rxf7+ Kb8

    24.Re6 Rd8

25.c4 Qc6

26.Ne5

The Bishop is pinned, so the Knight joins in the attack.

26...Qc8

27.Qb1!

Black resigns. He cannot allow 28.Qxb6+, but 27...b5 28.cxb5 Bxe5 29.bxa6+ is the end. The attempt to defend the b6-pawn with 27...Bc7 fails to 28.Rxb6+! Ka7 (or 28...Bxb6 29.Qxb6+ Checkmate) 29.Nc6 Checkmate. Another one bites the dust!

PART 3

More Tests
and Solutions

As its title indicates, Part 3 starts with a series of tests. Unlike the tests in the chapters in Part 1, these tests are presented cold—I don't give you any clues about which tactics might be involved. Finding out whether checkmate is possible or whether the capture of a single pawn is the solution I'm looking for will cost you some moments of concentration, just as it would in a real game. As well as trying to solve the problem correctly, write down your answers, indicate the tactic associated with the problem, and note any variations that come to mind. Try to discover not only the best move, but also the best defense and how to win against that best move. Pursue the positions as far as you can.

So that you can judge how well you've done, I've assigned a point value to each of the tests in these chapters. When you have finished all the tests, look up the answers and calculate your score. You can then compare your total score to the evaluations at the end of Chapter Twenty-Five.

Basic Tactics

This chapter tests your grasp of basic tactics such as pins, forks, discovered attacks, skewers, and the like. The goal is to get your gray matter primed and ready for the more difficult challenges in Chapter Twenty-Two. Be sure to record your solutions. Good luck!

TEST 93. White to play.

TEST 94. White to play.

TEST 95. White to play.

TEST 96. Black to play.
Maric–Gligoric
Belgrade, 1962

TEST 97. White to play.
Böök–Saila
Stockholm, 1946

TEST 98. White to play.

199

TEST 99. White to play.
Study by A. White, 1919

TEST 100. White to play.
Seirawan–Korchnoi
Las Palmas, 1981

TEST 101. Black to play.
Dantas–Wexler
Mar del Plata, 1951

TEST 102. White to play.
Szabó–Ban
Budapest, 1947

TEST 103. Black to play.
Cohen–Seirawan
US Open, 1977

TEST 104. Black to play.
Kleist–Wilke
Saarbrücken, 1958

TEST 105. Black to play.
N. Weinstein–Seirawan
Montreal, 1977

TEST 106. White to play.
Toran–Kuypers
Malaga, 1965

TEST 107. White to play.
Petrosyan–Spassky
Moscow, 1966

Advanced Combinations

You should be nice and warmed up after Chapter Twenty-One. The following problems are considerably more difficult, so correct solutions earn more points. Once again, be sure to record your solutions and include as much insight into the position as you can.

TEST 108. White to play.
Seirawan–Bisguier
US Open, 1977

TEST 109. White to play.
Cudinovskih–Muravev
USSR, 1990

TEST 110. Black to play.
Przepiórka–Ahues
Kecskemet, 1927

TEST 111. White to play.
Fajbisovic–Etruk
USSR, 1975

TEST 112. Black to play.
C. Juarez–Lputian
Manila, 1990

TEST 113. Black to play.
Stepanov–Romanovsky
Leningrad, 1926

TEST 114. White to play.
Deep Thought–M. Lyon
New York, 1990

TEST 115. Black to play.
P. Meister–Brynell
London, 1990

TEST 116. White to play.
Seirawan–Arkell
London, 1981

TEST 117. White to play.
J. Polgar–L. Hansen
Vejstrup, 1989

TEST 118. White to play.
R. Byrne–Tarjan
Cleveland, 1975

TEST 119. Black to play.
Lefevre–Silman
Pasadena, 1990

TEST 120. White to play.
I. Figaro–Bjerring
Gausdal, 1989

TEST 121. White to play.
Alekhine–Nestor
Trinidad, 1939

TEST 122. White to play.
Bareev–Kupreichik
USSR, 1990

CHAPTER TWENTY-THREE

Professional Combinations

If you've made it this far through the test chapters, you are clearly the kind of player who enjoys a challenge. Well, let me warn you: The tests in this chapter are tough, and I do mean tough. When you've completed the tests, add up your score to see how tactically gifted you are.

TEST 123. White to play.
Shankarananda–Ashton
Santa Monica, 1991

TEST 124. White to play.
P.F. Schmidt–P.R.Schmidt
Heidelberg, 1946

TEST 125. White to play.
Seirawan–Zaltsman
New York, 1987

TEST 126. White to play.
Rossolimo–Reissman
San Juan, 1967

TEST 127. White to play.
Study by A. Kakovin, 1961

TEST 128. Black to play.
Bannik–Cherepkov
USSR, 1961

**TEST 129. White to play.
Study by Mandler
and I. Konig, 1924**

**TEST 130. Black to play.
Liddel–Silman
San Diego, 1971**

**TEST 131. White to play.
Study by S. Kaminer, 1935**

**TEST 132. White to play.
Study by V. and M. Platov,
1907**

TEST 133. White to play.

**TEST 134. Black to play.
Tal–Bohnisch
Berlin, 1969**
Is 1...Rxc3 a strong move
for Black?

**TEST 135. White to play.
Oskam–NN
Rotterdam, 1927**

**TEST 136. Black to play.
Rotlewi–Rubinstein
Lodz, 1907**

**TEST 137. White to play.
Steinitz–Von Bardeleben
Hastings, 1895**

![checkered banner]

Solutions to Tests from Part 1

In this chapter, I have gathered together the solutions to the tests presented in Part 1. You shouldn't have any trouble understanding these answers. In each chapter, I gave lots of clues about what to look for, so I expect you will have done well.

Chapter Two Tests

TEST 1: No! **2.Ne1!** is a double attack on Black's Queen and Rook. Then **2...Qg5 3.Nxg2 Qxg2** wins the Exchange for a pawn (a 1-point advantage).

TEST 2: The surprising **1.Nxh4!** wins a pawn.

TEST 3: A classic pawn snatch: **1.Nxd4!**. Then 1...Nxd4 allows 2.Bxg4, whereas 1...Bxe2 2.Nxe2 keeps the pawn.

TEST 4: The stunning **1.Bg8!**, which threatens both the Queen and a check- mate on h7, is a winner for White.

TEST 5: Best is **1.Nf5!**, which threatens the Black Queen and opens up the White Queen's path to the checkmating h8-square. (In this case, a piece discovers an attack against a square instead of against a piece or pawn.)

TEST 6: The elegant solution is **1.Rc8! Rxa7.** The pawn must be captured; otherwise, a8=Q forces the capture of a Rook. Then **2.Kb6+** is a discovered check, which captures the Rook.

TEST 7: White plays the interference move **1.Bd8!,** which ends Black's protection of the a8-Rook and makes a discovered attack on the f7-pawn. For Black, 1...Raxd8 2.Qxf7+, 1...Rf8 2.Qxa8, and 1...Qf5 2.Qxa8 are all hopeless.

TEST 8: White plays **1.Rxf6!,** with a double threat of 2.Qxg4 and 2.Rg6+ (the dreaded double check). Black should play 1...Nxf6 2.Qxg4, even though this sequence leaves White with a Bishop and two pawns for the Exchange (full material equality), and the pin still causes Black great anguish. Instead, Black can't resist the bait offered on d1, and with **1...Bxd1?,** he chops off the White Queen. The conclusion is made possible by a double check: **2.Rg6++** (attacking Black's King with both the Bishop on b2 and the Rook on g6; note that the Rook on g6 is defended by the Bishop on d3) **2...Kh7 3.Rg7++** (another double discovered check, this time with the d3-Bishop as the Rook's partner) **3...Kh8** (the Rook can't be captured because of the protection of the b2-Bishop) **4.Rh7+ Kg8 5.Rh8** Checkmate. The brutal flurry of checks gives Black no chance to do anything but move his King!

TEST 9: Lured by the prospect of taking a pawn and attacking the Black Knight, White could play 1.Qxa4. Unfortunately, with 1...Qc7, Black can hold on. Emanual Lasker once said, "When you see a good move, you must sit on your hands and look for a better one." This bit of wisdom serves White well here. If he plays **1.Qd8+,** after **1...Kh7 2.Qxa5,** he wins a piece.

TEST 10: White wins with **1.Rxc6!,** snaring a pawn and drawing the defender away from the critical e7-square. Black can't take the Rook because 1...Rxc6 2.Ne7+ leads to a family fork.

TEST 11: As before, White can chop off the c-pawn with **1.Nxc6!,** after which 1...Qxc6? 2.Ne7+ captures the Queen. All well and good, but what happens if Black plays **1...Nxc6** instead, covering the e7-square with two pieces? White blasts this threat apart with **2.Qxc6! Qxc6 3.Ne7+,** recovering the Queen and ending up with an extra pawn.

TEST 12: White can start a series of checks that soon lead to a fork on the Black King and the loose a3-Bishop: **1.Qa8+ Kd7 2.Qc6+ Kc8 3.Qa6+**, which wins the Bishop. Don't forget Silman's Rules of Recognition:

> *When an enemy piece is undefended and the enemy King is weak, a tactical move has a good chance of success.*

TEST 13: The tempting 1.Qf5? threatens both the d7-Knight and a checkmate on h7. However, Black can parry both threats with 1...Nf6. So I played the forceful **1.Nxh7! Kxh7 2.Qf5+ Kg8 3.Qxd7**, which netted me an extra pawn and an eventual victory.

TEST 14: White found the exceedingly strong **1.Qc4!!**, which led to Black's immediate resignation! Because this move threatens Black's Rook on c8 and sets up 2.Qg8 Checkmate (it forks a Rook and a checkmating square), Black has no time to capture the loose White Rook on e8, and **1...Rxc4** is answered by **2.Rxf8** Checkmate.

TEST 15: Black creates a fork by giving his Queen away with **1...Qg1+!**, and White gives up. Why? Black's move forces the White King to retreat to the unfortunate g1-square with 2.Kxg1, after which Black can take a Bishop with 2...Nxe2+ and simultaneously fork the King and Queen. Because Black is then up a piece, White resigns.

TEST 16: I was able to fork White's Queen and Bishop with **1...Nce5!**. Then, when White's pawn takes one Knight off the board with **2.dxe5**, my other horse is able to take its place: **2...Nxe5 3.Qg3 Nxc4**. This combination leaves me with an extra pawn plus a good position, and I went on to win the game.

TEST 17: No! Playing **1...Qg5??** loses a piece because it walks right into a double discovered attack. After **2.d4!**, Black's Bishop hangs to the d4-pawn, and the Black Queen is attacked by the c1-Bishop.

TEST 18: White's b6-pawn is blocked by its Black counterpart on b7. Seeing that the pawn advance would be strong, White plays **1.Rxc6+!**. Then **1...bxc6 2.b7+** leads to a fork that immediately regains the Rook and leaves White with an extra piece for a pawn (a 2-point advantage).

TEST 19: White plays a combination that depends on many factors for its ultimate success: **1.Rxc8!+ Rxc8** (1...Kxc8 is impossible because of 2.Rxe8+; note that the Knight on e8 needs to be carefully watched) **2.d7!** (a pawn fork) **2...Kxd7** (a forced capture, but now Black's King is on the same diagonal as his Rook) **3.Bg4+** (skewering the King and Rook) **3...Kd8 4.Bxc8**. White is now up an Exchange and a pawn (a 3-point advantage) because 4...Kxc8 hangs the Knight on e8.

Chapter Three Tests

TEST 20: With **1.Qh5+**, White puts an end to the fight. Black cannot capture the White Queen because the d3-Bishop is pinning the g6-pawn. After **1...Kg7**, Black is wiped off the board with **2.Qxg6+ Kh8 3.Qh7** Checkmate.

TEST 21: I'm willing to sacrifice a Rook and a Knight in order to achieve the position shown in Test 20: **1.Rxh7! Kxh7?** (in the actual game, Black played 1...f5, and after 2.Rh1, I was a pawn ahead and eventually won) **2.Ng5+** (having pulled Black's King to the vulnerable h7-square, I sacrifice another piece to make way for my Queen) **2...fxg5** (better is 2...Kg8, but then 3.Nxe6 gets back all my material plus dividends of a pawn) **3.Qh5+** (notice the similarities between Test 21 and Test 20; the Black King will be checkmated because his pinned pawn cannot capture the White Queen) **3...Kg7 4.Qxg6+ Kh8 5.Qh7** Checkmate. As this example shows, no material price is too much to pay if it enables you to force a checkmate!

TEST 22: White has to play **1.Kh1**. If he plays 1.Bd4??, he loses a piece because this Bishop is then pinned to the King, making 1...Qxe5! possible.

TEST 23: Black's **1...Qd4??** is a blunder that immediately loses to **2.Rd1!**. Black then has two hopeless possibilities: 2...Qxc3 3.Rxd7+ followed by 4.bxc3, or 2...e5 3.Rxd4. Black should have played 1...Kg8, which produces a defendable position.

TEST 24: White creates an absolute pin by temporarily sacrificing his Queen: **1.Qxf8+! Kxf8 2.Ne6+** (forking Black's King and Queen; Black can't play 2...Nxe6 because his Knight is pinned to his King) **2...Kf7 3.Nxd8+**. White wins the Exchange for a 2-point advantage.

TEST 25: White's 1.Qxa7 is a pretty strong move, but he can smash Black completely with **1.Rd8+!** because the forced **1...Kxd8** creates a pin on the Knight (the Black Queen's only defender). After **2.Qxc6**, Black gives up. This example demonstrates an important principle:

A piece that is suffering under an absolute pin can't defend anything.

TEST 26: Warning: Even absolute pins can be broken! After the blunder **1...Qxf6??**, White plays **2.Rxc5!**. Suddenly Black's pin is gone! Notice that 2...bxc5 is a bad idea because of 3.Bxf6, so Black must move his Queen and accept the loss of a piece.

TEST 27: Far from it! Black loses a whole Knight to **1.Qxe4!**, which makes use of the pin against Black's d5-pawn. If Black defends his Queen, the White Queen retreats to safety, and 1...dxe4 2.Rxd7 is also quite hopeless for Black.

TEST 28: If you said "Yes," then you fell for my trap! Making use of the relative pin on the b1–h7 diagonal with **1.Nxg4??** looks promising (the f5-pawn can't move because of Bxg6) until Black bashes you with **1...Bh5!** and an absolute counter-pin! White's shortsighted greed then costs him his Knight.

TEST 29: Though White's e5-Knight seems to be solidly defended, I demonstrated its vulnerability by playing **1...Nxf4! 2.Rxf4 Bxe5**. (The d4-pawn can't capture my Bishop because of the pin on the d-file.) I am now up a pawn, and White's d4-pawn and f4-Rook are under fire. After **3.Re4 Bf6 4.Rf1 c5** (taking advantage of the new pin on the a1–h8 diagonal) **5.Qd2 cxd4**, White resigns.

TEST 30: White can play the very strong **1.Rxf6! Nxf6 2.Bg5**, pinning Black's Knight to his Rook and threatening 3.Bxf6, which wins a piece. Because Black has no way to defend this Knight, he will have to accept the loss of two pieces for a Rook (a loss of 1 point).

TEST 31: After **1.Rxf6! Nxf6 2.Bg5**, Black is able to step out of the relative pin with **2...Rd6** and simultaneously defend his Knight. Ordinarily, this defense might be adequate, but here Black is unlucky. White can create a new absolute pin with **3.Bf4!** and meet 3...Ne8, 3...Ne4, or 3...Kc7 with 4.c5, which leaves White with an extra piece.

TEST 32: No. Creating a pin with **1.Bb5** (and threatening the winning 2.Qa4) fails to put Black away because the defensive **1...Qa8!** breaks the pin and still defends the Knight.

TEST 33: Because the c6-Knight is pinned and cannot move without a major loss of material, White's goal is to find a way to force it to jump. With this in mind, White plays **1.Ba4!**, threatening 2.b5. Black is forced to shed a pawn to meet this threat: **1...b5**. Play continues with **2.Bxb5 Ke8** (Black intends to bring his King to d8, where it can give extra support to the c7-Rook, thus breaking the pin on the c-file) **3.Ba4** (again threatening 4.b5) **3...Kd8 4.h4!**. Now 4.b5 no longer accomplishes anything because either 4...Na5 or 4...Nb8 adequately protects the c7-Rook. But suddenly it becomes clear that Black is in *zugzwang*—he is compelled to move, but any move he makes will worsen his position. Black would like to say "Pass," but cannot legally do so.

He has to move something. He can't move the e7-Knight without hanging the other c6-Knight. He can't move the c6-Knight because Bxd7 loses the Queen. If he moves either of his Rooks, Bxc6 picks up the Knight. And if he plays 4...Ke8 or 4...Qe8, White will play 5.b5 for a deadly pin along the c-file. The best choice for Black is pawn moves on the Kingside, but he would eventually run out of these and be forced to make a self-destructive move. With these grim thoughts running through his mind, Black resigns the game. (All he has to do is tip over his King, shake hands, and his problems are solved!)

This position is a wonderful example of the power of a pin along an open file and of how the doubling of Rooks (or even tripling, with the Queen, as we saw here) increases the pin's strength.

Chapter Four Tests

TEST 34: Though White has a strong skewer available with 1.Bb3+ followed by 2.Bxf7, this move turns out to be only second best. Correct is the game ending **1.Qf5** Checkmate! Just because you have the opportunity for a powerful skewer, pin, or fork doesn't mean you have to play it. Take your time and look for something even better. The skewer, pin, or fork won't run away while you're scouting around.

TEST 35: White can take his pick of skewers. Both **1.Be8** followed by the capture of one of the Rooks and **1.Ra5+ Kd6 2.Rxh5 Kxd7** leave White with a one-pawn advantage.

TEST 36: White has three different skewer possibilities. He can play 1.Qc2+, skewering Black's King and Bishop; or 1.Qe2+, skewering Black's King and Rook; or 1.Qg2+, skewering Black's King and Queen. White should play **1.Qg2+** because the Queen is the most valuable piece. Note that 1.Qb4+ wins the Black Rook but is a fork, not a skewer.

Chapter Five Tests

TEST 37: Black plays **1...Rc4+!**, which forces **2.Qxc4**. The White Queen then takes away all of the Black King's remaining squares. As you can see, your King does not have to start out in a stalemated position. By bringing your opponent's pieces closer to your King, you can make your opponent create the stalemate himself by taking away the only squares that were available to your King. But be careful when creating stalemates. You can easily set yourself up for a checkmate instead!

TEST 38: The first idea is poor, but the mystery move is **1.Bd4+!**, which forks Black's King and Bishop and forces **1...Bxd4**, stalemating White's King and ensuring a draw.

TEST 39: It is a big mistake because White can now save the game with **2.Qxg5+!**, forcing 2...fxg5, which makes the h4-square uninhabitable. Also note that the g3-pawn can't move because it's pinned by the Black Queen. Instead of the terrible 1...Rg5??, Black could have played 1...Qh5+ (getting rid of all stalemate possibilities once and for all) 2.Kg2 Qd5+. Then a forced exchange of Queens leads to an easily won endgame. The exchanging of pieces when ahead in force is called *simplification*. When you have a large advantage in material, trading pieces is often a good strategy because you destroy your opponent's hopes of counterplay. Because Black is on the attack, an even better approach than simplification is 1...Kg7!, which makes 2...Rh6+ unstoppable.

TEST 40: The attractive **1...b2??** is a blunder. True, after **2.Rxb2 Rh2+**, Black wins a Rook, but he forgets that **3.Kf3 Rxb2** will result in a stalemate!

TEST 41: No. White can win with **2.Kg3 Qe1+ 3.Kg4**, when he escapes the checks. Taking the Queen leads to a stalemate after 2.Kxh1?? b1=Q+ 3.Kh2 Qh1+! 4.Kg3 (4.Kxh1 is an immediate stalemate) 4...Qxg2+!, which forces White to capture Black's remaining piece. A draw follows.

TEST 42: White is hoping for **2...Qxg3??**, when suddenly his King is stalemated and all he needs to do is jettison his remaining two pieces. He plays **3.Qg8+! Kxg8 4.Rxg7+!**. Now 4...Kxg7 or 4...Qxg7 leads to a stalemate, and 4...Kf8 5.Rf7+! Ke8 6.Re7+! also gets Black nowhere. White will keep offering the Rook until a stalemate occurs.

TEST 43: It's checkmate after **1.Qxh7+! Bxh7** (this Bishop can't move now because it is pinned by the Rook on h1) **2.Ng6**. Note that the immediate 1.Ng6+ Bxg6 fails.

TEST 44: White draws immediately by playing **1.Re8+ Rxe8 2.Qxe8+ Kh7 3.Qh5+ Kg8 4.Qe8+**, forcing a repetition.

TEST 45: Black's King cannot cross over the d-file boundary because of White's Rook on d5. The King also happens to be trapped on the 1st rank because of White's other Rook on h7. White can draw by using his Knight to harass the Black King: **1.Nf6+ Kf8 2.Nd7+ Kg8 3.Nf6+**, and so on.

TEST 46: Black can force a draw with **1...Nxg5!** (preparing a forced entry into White's King position) **2.hxg5 Nxd5!!** (creating a double attack). Black now threatens 3...Nxc3 or 3...Qxg5+. The first threat is more troublesome, so White must capture the Black Knight. Play continues with **3.Nxd5 Qxg5+ 4.Kh1 Qh4+ 5.Kg1 Qg5+ 6.Kh1**, producing a draw.

TEST 47: Black has a pretty way to save himself with **1...Rxh2+! 2.Kg1** (White would lose after 2.Kxh2? Rxf2+, with a quick checkmate) **2...Qxg3+!** (a nice way to connect the Rooks on the 7th rank) **3.fxg3 Rag2+ 4.Kf1 Rf2+** resulting in a draw.

TEST 48: Kick the door open with **1.Qxh7+! Kxh7 2.Rh3** Checkmate.

TEST 49: White gets crushed by **1...Qxg3+!** because after **2.Kxg3**, the King's cover is destroyed and the King is in a vulnerable position with few available moves. When the d8-Bishop joins in with **2...Bh4**, the game is over because checkmate has been called!

TEST 50: White starts to sacrifice his pieces in an effort to expose the Black King: **1.Rxf6! gxf6 2.Qg4** (threatening to move the g6-Knight for a strong discovered check) **2...f5** (attacking the Queen and attempting to keep the White Rook out of the battle. Black avoids 2...fxe5 3.Nxe5+ Kh8 4.Nf7 Checkmate) **3.Ne7++** (White's Queen is still safe because Black's King is in a double check) **3...Kf8 4.Nxf5!!** (tearing down the wall). Now White's remaining pieces will hunt down Black's undefended King: **4...Bxf5 5.Rxf5+!** (material no longer matters because White wants checkmate and nothing but checkmate!) **5...exf5 6.Qxf5+ Ke7 7.Qf7+ Kd6 8.Qd7** Checkmate (or 6...Kg7 7.Qg6+ Kh8 8.Nf7 Checkmate). A good demonstration of the power of the discovered check!

TEST 51: By sacrificing my Rook with **1...Rxc2+!**, I strip White's King of all protection. Play continues like this: **2.Kxc2 Rc8+ 3.Nc3** (the King's stroll with 3.Kd3 fails to 3...Qb5+ 4.Ke3 Qxa4, when I have full material equality plus a very strong attack. Play with this position to understand why White's King is not happy. One possible sequence is 5.Kf2 Rc2 6.Qd3 Qf4+, and a win for Black) **3...d4 4.Rb1 Qc6!** (building the pressure against the c3-Knight) **5.Rb3 Nd5** (bringing the Knight into the battle and continuing to bash away at the c3-Knight) **6.Nb1 Bg4!** (now all my pieces are taking part in the fight) **7.Qh2** (the Bishop is taboo: 7.Qxg4?? Ne3+ forks the King and Queen) **7...dxc3**. I now have complete material equality (a Bishop plus two pawns, worth a total of 5 points, vs. a Rook, also worth 5 points) and a very strong attack (...Bf5+ is in the air). I will win in a few more moves.

TEST 52: By sacrificing his Queen, White forces the Black King to embark on a death march: **1.Qxh7+!! Kxh7 2.Nxf6++** (the Knight can't be captured because the King is attacked by both the Knight and the Bishop—a double check) **2...Kh6** (stepping back with 2...Kh8 is not advisable because the King is then stalemated, and any check, such as 3.Ng6, is checkmate) **3.Neg4+ Kg5 4.h4+ Kf4 5.g3+ Kf3** (a noble gesture, but it's very unusual for a King to lead its whole army into battle because the front line faces the fiercest fights—here, the King turns out to be the first major casualty)

6.Be2+ Kg2 7.Rh2+ Kg1 8.Kd2 Checkmate. The White King is not actually delivering checkmate here. It merely steps out of the way of the Rook on a1. Thus, we have a very rare discovered checkmate. Heed the warning: This fate often awaits adventurous Kings!

TEST 53: Black loses after **1...Rxa2** because the e8-square is covered only twice. After **2.Qxc7! Qxc7 3.Re8**, White conquers the back rank for checkmate. A much safer first move for Black is 1...g6, when White has to take the threat of 2...Rxa2 seriously. Best of all is 1...Ne6! blocking the e-file, preparing ...Ra8xa2.

TEST 54: A terrible move is **1...Qxa2?**, which allows **2.Ra1**. The Queen is then pinned and lost. If Black tries to wriggle free with a move like **2...Qxb2**, White plays **3.Ra8** for a back rank checkmate.

TEST 55: This time it doesn't work! After **1.Qe8+ Rxe8 2.Rxe8+**, Black can safely block the check with **2...Bf8**, when White has insufficient compensation for his sacrificed Queen.

TEST 56: The greedy pawn grab **1...Qxa2??** loses to **2.Qe8+! Rxe8** (2...Bf8 3.Qxd8 leaves White with an extra Rook) **3.Rxe8+ Bf8 4.Bh6!**. The pin means Black is powerless to prevent **5.Rxf8** Checkmate.

Chapter Six Tests

TEST 57: White can win a pawn with **1.Nxe5!** because Black's Bishop is overworked as the sole defender of both the pawn and the Knight. After **1...Bxe5**, White has successfully lured the defender away from the Knight, and **2.Rxb4** safely recaptures the piece.

TEST 58: With **1...Qe3!**, Black wins at once. The idea is to pull the Rook from its important defensive post on h3. White resigns because 2.Rxe3 allows 2...Rh2+ followed by 3...Reg2 Checkmate, and 2.Rxf2 succumbs to 2...Qxh3+ 3.Kg1 Qg3+ 4.Rg2 Qxg2 Checkmate. Note that 2.Rh4 Qf3+ is also deadly.

TEST 59: By deflecting the Queen of course! With a little thought, you should be able to come up with **1.Rxc8!**, which draws the Queen away from the protection of the f6-Bishop. Black resigns rather than face **1...Qxc8 2.Nxf6+** (I already have a lead of 6 points vs. 5, but to top it off I am forking Black's King and Rook) **2...Kg7 3.Nxd7**, and I will end up with an extra piece.

TEST 60: With **1.Bd5!**, I brought my extra piece into the attack. This move threatens some big discovered checks, attacks Black's Rook, and attempts to draw the Queen away from the protection of the e8-square (1...Qxd5 leads to 2.Qe8 Checkmate). Black replies with **1...Rg4+ 2.Kf2 Qc5** (preventing the possibility of 3.Qe8 by pinning my Queen to my King) **3.Rxc7+!**. Black resigns. He can save his Queen with 3...Qxd5, but then my Queen is freed from the pin, and 4.Qe8 Checkmate follows.

TEST 61: White can snuff out all resistance with **1.Rb8!!** and the threat of 2.Qg7 Checkmate. (The Rook can't take the Queen because it's pinned.) Black has no good answer to this move because 1...Rxb8 allows 2.Qg7 Checkmate, and 1...Qxb8 runs into 2.Nxf7 Checkmate.

Chapter Seven Tests

TEST 62: White wins with **1.Nxc6! bxc6 2.Rxd7**, for an extra pawn.

TEST 63: White can win a pawn with **1.Nb6! axb6 2.axb6.** The defender is forced to run away with **2...Rcc8**. After **3.Rxd7 Rxd7 4.Qxd7 Qxd7 5.Rxd7,** White also enjoys a Rook on the 7th. Though this play is excellent for White, even stronger is 1.b4!, which leaves Black powerless to prevent 2.Nc5 (1...b6 2.axb6 axb6 3.Nxb6 is no help). By exploiting the pin in this way, White makes even greater gains.

TEST 64: White should activate his Rook with **1.Rd1!**, taking over the all-important d-file and threatening to win a Knight with **2.Rd7+**, which forks the King and Knight. If White plays the slow and cowardly 1.a4 to free the

Rook from its duties as defender of the a-pawn, then 1...Rd8 enables Black to claim rights to the d-file.

TEST 65: If you tried 1.Rxh5 hoping for 1...gxh5?? 2.Qxh7 Checkmate, you lose any brownie points you might have gained from previous tests because Black plays 1...Nxd3+ and your Bishop disappears from the board with check! Then 2.Kb1 gxh5 3.Rxh5 allows 3...f5, when the Queen defends the h7-pawn from c7. The correct answer is the surprising **1.Qxh7+!!**, to which Black responds **1...Kxh7**. White has created a pin along the b1–h7 diagonal that allows him to blast open the h-file with gain of tempo. After **2.Rxh5+**, Black can't take the Rook because his g6-pawn is pinned by the Bishop. Black is checkmated after **2...Kg7 3.Rh7+ Kg8 4.Rh8+ Kg7 5.R1h7**. In this contest of attacks (Black threatens Nxd3), White triumphs because all his moves come with check.

TEST 66: White can win a whole piece with **1.Rxc6!** because **1...Bxc6?** allows **2.Bc4+ Bd5 3.Bxd5** Checkmate.

TEST 67: Playing **1...Bxa4** wins a piece and stops the threatened Knight fork. Normally, this move would be ideal but it doesn't take White's tactical threats along the a2–g8 and a1–h8 diagonals into account. White forces checkmate with **2.Qxf6+! Bxf6 3.Bxf6**.

TEST 68: This position is almost identical to the one in Test 67. In that case, White won by placing his Queen on c3 and forcing checkmate on the long diagonal. Here, White needs to get his Knight out of the way to do the same thing. After the unfortunate **1...b5?**, White delightedly plays **2.Nxb5!**. Black doesn't have time for **2...axb5** because **3.Qc3** produces an inevitable checkmate.

TEST 69: White eradicates all life on Black's side of the board with **1.Rxe7!!** (a clearance sacrifice—the Rook blocked White's real intentions so he throws it to the winds—see Chapter Ten for a more detailed explanation on this tactic) **1...Qxe7 2.Qxc6+! bxc6 3.Ba6** Checkmate.

Chapter Eight Tests

TEST 70: Black wins after **1...Bxg3! 2.hxg3 h2**, when his h-pawn is crowned.

TEST 71: By sacrificing his Rook with **1.Rh5!!**, White is able to pull Black's Rook away from the White pawns. Black gives up because after 1...Rxh5 2.fxe7, he cannot stop 3.e8=Q.

TEST 72: White turns his f-pawn into an unstoppable passed pawn after **1.Qc8+ Kh7 2.Qxe6!**. Black is down a Rook after **2...fxe6 3.f7,** and a new Queen is about to be born. He gives up.

TEST 73: Strangely enough, Black actually wins this position! He can initiate a breakthrough combination with **1...f4! 2.exf4** (2.gxf4 h4! followed by 3...h3 leads to a quick Queen) **2...h4!** (threatening to queen with 3...h3 and then win) **3.gxh4 g3! 4.fxg3 e3**. White resigns because Black can crown a new Queen. (You might want to compare this position with the one in Diagram 87.)

TEST 74: No, Black could force a draw after 1.f8=Q?? with Qg5+!, when no matter how the Queen is captured, a stalemate results. Correct is **1.f8=R!**, when White's huge material advantage (14 points vs. 9 points) leads to eventual victory. For example, after 1...Qh6+ 2.Kg4 Qg6+ 3.Kh3, Black runs out of checks. Or 1...Qd1+ 2.Rf3 Qd5+ 3.R8f5 Qd1 (pinning the Rook on f3) 4.Rf7+ Kg8 5.Kg6 Qb1+ 6.R3f5 leads to 7.Rf8+ and a win.

TEST 75: Most people would play 1.c8=Q??, but this move leads to a draw after 1...Qf7+, which forks White's King and Rook. Instead of blindly pursuing a new Queen, you can secure an easy win with **1.c8=N+!**, when White's new Knight scores a royal fork!

TEST 76: By using an underpromotion tactic, White achieves a winning endgame: **1.Rc8+! Rxc8 2.Qxa7+!! Kxa7 3.bxc8=N+! Kb7 4.Nxe7**, and White has two extra pawns.

Chapter Nine Tests

TEST 77: If Black's Queen were farther away, Black's King would not be able to support it. White engineers the breakup with **1.Rd8! Qxd8**. With the Queen out of the King's reach, White has created a skewer; and **2.Qh8+ Kf7 3.Qxd8** wins the Queen. After **3...g5 4.Rh6**, Black gives up.

TEST 78: White's Queen stops me from playing Qf3, so I first give up my Rook with **1...Rc1!** to put an end to the Queen's guard duty of the f3-square. After **2.Qxc1** (2.Qxg4 is impossible because White's Queen is pinned to his King), I can finally put my Queen where I want it with **2...Qf3+**. White can't face 3.Kg1 Nh3 Checkmate, so he resigns.

TEST 79: White can force checkmate by luring Black's King forward with **1.g5+! Kxg5 2.Qf4**.

TEST 80: Desperate measures are clearly called for because White will checkmate Black as soon as he gets a free move. Black wants to get his Bishop to f3, so he plays **1...Qh1+!!**, forcing White's King to the unfortunate h1-square. After **2.Kxh1 Bf3+**, Black puts his Bishop on f3 with a check and a gain of tempo. White is the one to be checkmated after **3.Kg1 Rd1**.

Chapter Ten Tests

TEST 81: Attacking the Bishop with 1...Ne7 gets Black nowhere because 2.Be4 or 2.Ba4 breaks the pin. If the b4-pawn were not in the way, Black could play 1...Nb4, forking the Queen and Bishop. If it's in the way, get rid of it! Black plays **1...b3!**, and White resigns, knowing that 2.axb3 Nb4 forks the Queen and Bishop.

TEST 82: White sees that his Bishop needs the c7-square if his upcoming attack on Black's King is to be successful. Because his Rook is in the way, he forces Black to take it by playing **1.Rc6+!**, which leads to **Bxc6 2.Nc5+ Ka5 3.Bc7** Checkmate.

TEST 83: White gets his Queen off the important h6-square with **1.Qe6+!**, after which either **1...Nxe6** or **1...Bxe6** are met by **2.Nh6** Checkmate.

Chapter Eleven Tests

TEST 84: A big check awaits on the c1-square, based on the weakness of White's back rank. Black can knock White out with **1...Bxa4!!** (opening up the c8-Rook with a gain of tempo so that it can x-ray through to c1) **2.Qxa4 Qc1+! 3.Rxc1 Rxc1+ 4.Qd1.** Usually White would resign at this point. By playing on, White hopes for one of four things to happen: Black loses on time; Black falls into a long-lasting, drug-induced sleep (the moral here is to never accept refreshments from your opponent); Black drops dead (believe it or not, this happens from time to time at chess tournaments, and to die at the chessboard is actually an ideal way to go for many chess fanatics); or reality as we know it comes to an end. In the absence of these setbacks, Black is free to conclude with **4...Rxd1** Checkmate.

TEST 85: Yes, he can. With **1...Nxd3!**, Black wins an important pawn, and with 2...c4, he intends to cement his Knight on the d3-square. If White tries to take the Knight with **2.Rxd3**, Black wins with a nice x-ray: **2...Qxd1+! 3.Qxd1** (3.Rxd1 leads to Rxd1+ 4.Qxd1 Rxd1 Checkmate) **3...Rxd3.** Now both **4.Qe2 Rd1+** and **4.Qf1 Rd1** lead to the capture of White's Queen and a subsequent Rook vs. Bishop advantage (2 points).

TEST 86: White can create a windmill with **1.Qxg7+! Nxg7 2.Rxg7+ Kh8 3.Rxd7+ Kg8 4.Rg7+ Kh8 5.Rxb7+ Kg8 6.Rxb2**, after which White is suddenly up a full piece!

TEST 87: White could set up a windmill with **1.Qe7+! Nxe7 2.Rxe7+ Qb7 3.Rxb7+ Ka8 4.Rxb5+ Ka7 5.Rb7+ Ka8 6.Rd7+ Kb8 7.Rxd1**, after which Black has lost all his pieces.

Chapter Thirteen Tests

TEST 88: Strangely enough, 1.Qxb7 leads to a forced draw because Black is able to create a perpetual pursuit of the White Queen. After **1...Rb8 2.Qxc6 Rc8 3.Qa6 Ra8 4.Qb5 Rb8**, Black simply continues to attack the White Queen until the draw is agreed upon.

TEST 89: If White plays **1.e4??**, Black creates a blockade with **1...dxe4 2.dxe4 Nxe4+! 3.fxe4 Rxe4**, followed by ...Rc4 and ...Ra4. Then White's King can never get over the 4th-rank barrier.

TEST 90: White can squeeze a draw by giving up his remaining piece to create a fortress: **1.Ba7+!! Rxa7 2.b6 Ra8 3.Kc3** (having completely closed the Queenside, White must rush over to the other wing and try to keep the enemy Rook from penetrating on the g-file) **3...Bxg4 4.Kd2 Kc8 5.Ke1 Kd7 6.Kf1 Rg8 7.Kg1! Bh5+ 8.Kh1!**. The game is a draw because neither the Black King nor the Bishop can penetrate White's position, and if the Black Rook stays on the g-file with 8...Rg2, the game ends in stalemate.

TEST 91: With **1...Bxf5! 2.Kxf5 Kh8**, Black can reach a basic draw. See Diagram 121 for a detailed explanation.

TEST 92: Show White that you had it all worked out and were never really in trouble by playing **1...Nxg4! 2.Nxg4 Bxg4 3.Kxg4 Kf6** followed by ...Kg7 and ...Kh8. The game is a draw because the h-pawn is crowned on the opposite color to the Bishop. Review the position in Diagram 123 for a reminder of why White cannot win here.

CHAPTER TWENTY-FIVE

Solutions to Tests from Part 3

The tests in Part 3 are different from those in Part 1. First, they are far more difficult and have no clues explaining which tactics to look for. Second, they are part of a larger picture. As you read the following solutions, you'll notice that I've assigned each problem a certain number of points, and I suggest that you keep a written record of your score. At the end of this chapter is a chart you can use to determine how well you absorbed the information I presented.

No matter how you fared, I hope this book has helped you appreciate the beautiful world of tactics and combinations and that you will one day produce your own brilliancies.

Chapter Twenty-One Tests

TEST 93: Here we have two themes: back rank checkmate and destruction of a defender. White checkmates with **1.Qxd6+!** (destroying the defender of e8) **1...Qxd6 2.Re8**. Value: 1 point.

TEST 94: Black's undefended Queen enables White to launch a discovered attack with **1.Bh7+! Kxh7 2.Qxd4**, after which White's material advantage should give him an easy victory. Value: 1 point.

TEST 95: This position demonstrates two kinds of forks. White is doubled on the c-file, but at the moment, this file is blocked. After **1.Bxe5+!** (which forks the King and Rook), White opens the c-file with a gain of tempo.

Black can now choose between the loss of the Exchange with 1...Kg8 2.Bxb8, or the loss of the Queen with 1...Nxe5 2.Rc7+ (which forks the King and Queen). Value: 2 points.

TEST 96: At a glance, things look hopeless for Black. He is down an Exchange, and his pawn structure is awful. White is hoping for 1...Qxf5? 2.Qxc3, with which he would technically win the game. Unfortunately for White, he forgets that his back rank is weak and his Queen is undefended. He gives up after **1...Rb3!!** because 2.axb3 Qxd2 and 2.Qc1 Rxb1 3.Qxb1 Qxf5 give Black a decisive material advantage. (Both 2.Qxa5 Rxb1+ and 2.Rd1 Qxd2 3.Rxd2 Rb1+ lead to checkmate.) Value: 2 points.

TEST 97: Here we have another back rank situation. If Black's Queen were not defending his Rook, then Rxf8 would be checkmate. With this in mind, White plays **1.Qe5!**, with the double threat of 2.Qxg7 Checkmate and 2.Qxc5, which grabs a Queen. Black has to resign because 1...Qxe5 takes his Queen away from his Rook and allows 2.Rxf8 Checkmate. Value: 2 points.

TEST 98: A hasty player might slide home with 1.c8=Q?? and expect his opponent to give up. However, Black's King would then be stalemated and the shocking 1...Qxb2+!! would deliver both a draw and a harsh dose of reality. White sees this possibility and makes a point of freeing the Black King and stopping any stalemates with **1.Rc4!**. Then Black cannot prevent **2.c8=Q**. Value: For 1.c8=Q??, –1point; for 1.Rc4, 2 points.

TEST 99: This position is silly, but it is a good demonstration of the power of a double check. Believe it or not, just 12 moves produce a forced checkmate, as follows: **1.Rf2++ Ke3 2.Rf3++ Ke4 3.Re3++ Kd4 4.Re4++ Kd5 5.Rd4++ Kc5 6.Rd5++ Kc6 7.Rc5++ Kb6 8.Rc6++ Kb7 9.Rb6++ Ka7 10.Rb7++ Ka8 11.Ra7++ Kb8 12.Ra8** Checkmate. Value: 1 point. I can hear you moaning about this meager earning, but White's moves are all forced, so you really should have figured this one out.

TEST 100: I am down a Rook, but I have a forced win because Black's Queen is unprotected. The first thing I must do is regain my Rook with gain of tempo by means of a zwischenzug: **1.Qf8+ Ka7 2.Qxc5+.** Now Black must lose material: **2...Ka8** (2...Kb8 leads to 3.Qxe5+, which picks up a pawn and the Knight) **3.Qc8+.** Black resigns because 3...Ka7 4.Nb5+ followed by Qxc2 loses his Queen. Value: 2 points. For 1.Qxc5??, –1 point, because then White loses to 1...Qxb2+! 2.Kxb2 Nd3+ when the fork leaves Black with a winning ending.

TEST 101: Black must avoid becoming entranced by the fact that his Queen is hanging because with **1...Rf2** he can force a win. White resigns because 2.Qxe1 Rh2 is checkmate. Value: 1 point.

TEST 102: All of Black's pieces are undefended, and his back rank is weak. Small wonder that White can find a tactic: **1.Qe5!.** Black gives up because 1...Qf6 2.Qxf4! Qxf4 3.Rd8+ is a quick checkmate (1...Qxe5 2.Rd8+ also leads to checkmate). Value: 1 point.

TEST 103: White's h6-Bishop is guarded once and attacked once. If I could play ...Qh4+, I would fork his King and Bishop, but at the moment my Knight is in the way. The answer then is to shove it aside with gain of tempo: **1...Nxe4! 2.Nxe4 Qh4+ 3.g3 Qxh6 4.0-0-0 Qxd2+.** My extra pawn eventually leads to the win. Value: 1 point.

TEST 104: White's threat of Rxf7+ is deadly. However, the simple **1...Qxf4!** destroys the pin and frees the Black pieces. After **2.gxf4,** Black can take advantage of the position of the White Queen by playing **2...Bg8.** The Queen is then trapped, and Black ends up with a decisive material advantage. Value: 2 points.

TEST 105: Whenever I see a King in the center, I look for possible checks against it. Here, I captured White's center pawns by creating the following fork: **1...Nxd4! 2.Nxd4 Qh4+ 3.g3 Qxd4,** with the e5-pawn next to fall. Value: 1 point.

TEST 106: White seems to be in trouble. He can't play 1.Bxg5 because his Bishop is pinned to his King. Another poor move is 1.Bxd4?? because Qxd2 captures the White Queen. The pins are a bother, but with **1.Qxd4!**, White can break them both. Black then resigns because 1...cxd4 2.Bxg5 leaves White with an extra piece. Value: 1 point.

TEST 107: With the pretty **1.Qh8+!**, White can create a fork. Black resigns because 1...Kxh8 2.Nxf7+ Kg7 3.Nxg5 leaves him with a hopeless endgame. Value: 1 point.

Chapter Twenty-Two Tests

TEST 108: The only thing stopping Qg5 Checkmate is Black's Queen, so White upsets Black's defense of this square with **1.Re5!**. Now 1...dxe5 allows 2.Qg5 Checkmate, so Black chooses an alternative: **1...Rb1+ 2.Kg2 Qxe5 3.Bxe5 dxe5 4.Qe4+ Kf6 5.f4!**. White wins in another ten moves. Value: 2 points.

TEST 109: White wins beautifully by first stalemating the Black King and then making use of a discovered-check tactic: **1.Rh8+!! Nxh8** (hemming in Black's King with his own Knight) **2.Qh7+!** (forcing Black's King onto the diagonal occupied by White's light-squared Bishop) **2...Kxh7 3.Rh5++** (forcing the King back into its stalemated hole with a double check) **3...Kg8 4.Bh7** Checkmate. Value: 3 points.

TEST 110: Black notices that with 1...Nf3, he can attack White's Queen. Unfortunately, White can simply move the Queen to safety. However, if White's King were on g1 or h2, then ...Nf3 would be a fork. Black's plan, then, is to force White's King onto one of the squares where the ...Nf3 fork can occur: **1...Rd1+ 2.Kg2 Rg1+!**. Now both 3.Kxg1 and 3.Kh2 allow 3...Nf3+ with a fork on the King and Queen, so White resigns. Value: 2 points.

TEST 111: The Black Rook on e7 is attacked once and defended once. If White could attack it just one more time, he could win it. With **1.Nxg6+!**, he gets what he wants. Now 1...Qxg6 leaves the Rook on e7 without a defender, and 1...hxg6 allows White to create a double-attack fork with 2.Qh4+. Then both the e7-Rook and the King are being hit, and Black is forced to part with the Rook, leaving White with a decisive material edge. So Black resigns. Value: 1 point.

TEST 112: By sacrificing a couple of pieces, Black can set up a checkmating threat against g2, which cannot be defended because of another checkmate by the Knight. Here's the play: **1...Rxd4!!** (taking away a defender from the f3-square) **2.cxd4 Bf3!** (threatening 3...Qxg2 Checkmate) **3.gxf3** (3.Rg1 leads to Nxf2 Checkmate—hardly a defense) **3...exf3** (4...Qg2 Checkmate is still a threat.) **4.Rg1** (the only defense) **4...Nxf2** Checkmate. Value: 4 points.

TEST 113: Seeing that White can't take on f3 because of a ...Nd4+ fork, Black hounds the White King so badly that he finally forces a fork, as follows: **1...d5+! 2.cxd5** (otherwise, 2.Kxf3 Nd4+ wins) **2..exd5+ 3.Kxd5 Be6+!** (trying for the same fork) **4.Kd6** (4.Kxc6 Rc8+ skewers White's Queen, whereas 4.Kxe6 Nd4+ is a royal fork) **4...Rd8+ 5.Kc7 Rf7+ 6.Kxc6 Rc8+ 7.Kd6 Rxc2.** Then Black's material advantage gives him an easy win. Value: 4 points.

TEST 114: The first part of the solution to this test is based on the fact that Black's c6-Knight cannot move without losing the Queen on a5. The final part is a fork at the end of the game. This is the solution: **1.Nde5+!! fxe5 2.Nxe5+ Kf6** (2...Ke7 loses to both 3.Nxc6+ and 3.Qxc6! Nxc6 4.Nxc6+, the winning move) **3.Qxa5 Nxa5 4.Rxb8! Rhxb8 5.Rxb8 Rxb8 6.Nd7+ Ke7 7.Nxb8.** White emerges with a winning endgame. Value: 5 points.

TEST 115: With Black's Bishop and Queen lined up on the long open diagonal, White's King is precariously placed. If Black could somehow open the a-file, then a Rook check would finish off the poor King. Black first sacrifices an Exchange with **1...Rexc7!** in order to make the a8-square available to the c8-Rook. Then **2.bxc7 Nb4+!** (forcing the opening of the a-file) **3.axb4 Ra8+ 4.Kb1 Ra1** achieves checkmate. Value: 4 points.

TEST 116: I won this game by setting Black up for a Bishop fork. Here's how: **1.fxe5! Bxe5** (1...fxe5? 2.Bg5+ forces the capture of material) **2.Nxb6! Nxb6 3.Bxc5+ Kd7 4.Bxb6**, and my material advantage leads to an easy win. Value: 3 points.

TEST 117: Both Kings are feeling the heat, and it's just a matter of which one will be the first to be checkmated. Seeing that Black threatens 1...Re4+, White realizes that she has no time for quiet moves. Aware of the power of doubled Rooks on the 7th, she plays **1.Qg7+! Kxg7 2.Rfxf7+** (doubling the Rooks on the 7th with tempo) **2...Kg8 3.Rg7+ Kh8 4.Rh7+ Kg8 5.Rbg7** Checkmate. Value: 3 points.

TEST 118: Black's Queen is undefended, making this combination possible: **1.Qh3!** (threatening 2.Qh7 Checkmate) **1...Kxf7 2.Qh7+ Ke8 3.Qh8+ Kd7 4.Qxb8**, and White wins. Value: 2 points.

TEST 119: Black would love to play 1...Qd1 Checkmate, but his Bishop is in the way. This neat space-clearing sacrifice enables Black to get his way: **1... Bf5!** (blocking the Queen's access to d1. Now both 2.Qxf5 and 2.Nxf5 lose to 2...Qd1 Checkmate) **2.Qf3 Bd3!+** (forcing the King to give up control of the e1-square). White resigns because both 3.Kg1 Re1 and 3.Qxd3 Qd1 are checkmate. Value: 2 points.

TEST 120: White sees the possibility of Rxb7+ Checkmate and heads right for it with **1.Rb1!**. Because 2.Qxb6 Checkmate is threatened and because 1...Qxc5 loses to 2.Rxb7 Checkmate, Black has no choice but to play **1...Nd7**, defending his Queen and attacking White's Queen on c5. Now the elegant **2.Qd4!** puts White's Queen out of the reach of Black's Knight and threatens 3.Rxb6. (Note that 3...Qxb1 is not possible because Black's Queen is pinned to his King.) With no further options left, Black gives in to the inevitable with **2...Qxd4 3.Rxb7** Checkmate. Value: 3 points.

TEST 121: The d-pawn is a big queening threat, and Black must also watch out for back rank checkmates. White takes advantage of these factors with **1.Rc8! Rxc8** (avoiding 1...Qxd7 2.Qf8+! Rxf8 3.Rxf8 Checkmate) **2.Qe7!!**. A stunning shot. White now threatens 3.Qxe6 followed by 4.dxc8=Q, and 2...Rg8 3.d8=Q Rxd8 4.Qxd8+ leads to checkmate. Taking the Queen with 2...Qxe7 also fails to 3.dxc8=Q+ and an eventual checkmate. Having no other options, Black resigns. Value: 3 points.

TEST 122: Based on the undefended state of the Black Queen, White has this shocking continuation: **1.Ne6!!** (threatening 2.Qg7 Checkmate) **1...N6h5** (defending the g7-square but leaving himself open for a quick checkmate; however, Black can't capture the impudent White Knight because 1...Nxe6 2.Qxd2 drops the Black Queen, and 1....fxe6 2.Rxg6+ Kf7 3.Rg7+ also leads to Black's demise) **2.Qf8+ Kh7 3.Ng5** Checkmate. Value: 3 points.

Chapter Twenty-Three Tests

TEST 123: White takes advantage of the stalemated Black King with **1.Qxg6!!** (threatening 2.Qf7 Checkmate). Black parries with **1...Nd6** (avoiding 1...hxg6 2.Nxg6 Checkmate). White takes off the h7-pawn with **2.Qxh7!**, making the g6-square available to his Knight. Black resigns because 2...Nxh7 3.Ng6 is checkmate. Value: 3 points.

TEST 124: White can force checkmate in nine moves by drawing Black's King out into the open. Here's how: **1.Qh6+!! Kxh6** (1...Kh8 leads to 2.Qxh7+! Kxh7 3.hxg6++ Kg7 4.Rh7+ Checkmate) **2.hxg6+ Kg5 3.Rh5+!** (a sacrifice that allows the f-pawn and the Bishop to join in the attack with gain of tempo) **3...Kxh5 4.f4+ Nxe2 5.Nf6+** (an important move that keeps Black's King away from g4) **5...Kh6 6.Rh1+ Kg7 7.Ne8+!** (drawing the Rook away from the defense of the f7-pawn) **7...Rxe8 8.Rxh7+ Kf6 9.Rxf7** Checkmate. Value: 4 points if you saw the whole scenario. Give yourself 1 point if you found 1.Qh6+, 2 points if you also found 3.Rh5+, and 3 points if you then found 4.f4+.

TEST 125: I had been playing for this position for some time. The audience was convinced that Black had everything defended, but I had this possibility of a Knight fork and an easy winning ending: **1.Bxe6+! Bxe6 2.Qf8+! Kxf8 3.Nxe6+ Ke7 4.Nxc7**. Now Black has the choice of losing his d5-pawn or protecting it with 4...Kd6, which allows 5.Ne8+, forking yet another pawn. Black chooses to resign instead. Value: 2 points.

TEST 126: White can pursue a powerful checkmating attack with **1.Nf6+** (stalemating the Black King) **1...Kh8 2.Qg6!!** (spectacular! White's Queen is hanging in two ways, and his Knight on f6 is also hanging. The immediate threat is 3.Qxh7 Checkmate) **2...Qc2** (defending the h7-pawn—all defenses by captures lose: 2...hxg6 3.Rh3 Checkmate; 2...fxg6 3.Nxg6+! hxg6 4.Rh3 Checkmate; and 2...gxf6 3.Qxf6+ Ng7 4.Rg3 Rg8 5.Nxf7+ picks up Black's Queen) **3.Rh3! Qxg6** (3...fxg6 is met by 4.Rxh7 Checkmate) **4.Nxg6+ fxg6 5.Rxh7** Checkmate. Value: 4 points. If you saw 1.Qg6, give yourself 1 point. If you also saw that all defenses by captures lose for Black, give yourself 2 points, and if you spotted the 2...Qc2 defense, give yourself 3 points.

TEST 127: White's Knight is trapped. He could give up his remaining pawn to save the Knight with 1.f5? Kg3 2.Ng6 Kg4 3.Ne7 Bxf5, producing a draw. However, by using the double-attack and discovered-check tactics, White can save everything and win the game. Here's how: **1.Bc7! Kg3 2.Ng6! Bxg6 3.f5+** (threatening both King and Bishop) **3...Kg4 4.fxg6**, giving White a new Queen. Value: 3 points.

TEST 128: A series of pins signals the end for White: **1...Rg5+ 2.Rg2 Qc5+ 3.Qf2** (3.Kh1 leads to Rh5+ 4.Rh2 Ree5!, after which the threat of 5...Rxh2+ followed by 6...Rh5 is decisive) **3...Re2!! 4.Rxg5** (4.Qxc5 results in Rgxg2+ 5.Kh1 Rh2+ 6.Kg1 Reg2 Checkmate) **4...Qxg5+**. White resigns. Value: 4 points.

TEST 129: At first, this position looks rather dull. There is no hint of suspense in the air. However, after **1.f7! Kg7 2.f8=Q+! Kxf8 3.Rf1+**, Black is lost because of this very nice pin: **3...Kg7** (playing 3...Ke7 means White wins a Rook with 4.Rfe1!) **4.Rg2+ Kh6 5.Rh1+ Rh3 6.Rgh2!**. White achieves his objective of winning a Rook. Value: 4 points.

TEST 130: Black uses two types of pins to attack the White King: **1...Ng4+! 2.hxg4 Qxg4** (threatening 3...Qh4+ Checkmate) **3.Bf1 Qh4+** (enjoying the fact that White's g3-Bishop is pinned to his King and that he can force another pin) **4.Bh3 Bd7** (exploiting the second pin) **5.Kh1 Bxg3 6.Rxg3 Qxg3 7.Bxd7 Qe1+ 8.Kh2 Qe2+**, the goal of the combination. After **9.Qxe2 fxe2**, Black crowns a new Queen. Note that this finish is a demonstration of the power of a passed pawn. Value: 4 points. Give yourself 2 points if you got as far as 4...Bd7, but you must have seen 8...Qe2+ at the end to get the full 4 points.

TEST 131: This very difficult combination is based on a series of pins and ends in a fork. The obvious 1.h8=Q?? Bxg6+ 2.Ka1 Be7! leads to a threat of 3...Bf6+, with a deadly attack. White cannot forestall this possibility with 3.Nf3 because 3...Bf6+ 4.Ne5+ Ke7 gives Black the better position. If White is to be successful, he must play the surprising **1.Nf4!!**. This suicidal-looking move draws the g-pawn away from the defense of the h4-square and allows White the possibility of this strange pin: **1...gxf4 2.h8=Q Bg6+ 3.Ka1 Be7 4.Nf3 Bf6+ 5.Ne5+ Ke7 6.Qxh4!!** (the goal of 1.Nf4: White's sixth move is not possible with Black's pawn on g5) **6...Bxh4** (forestalling 7.Qxf4 and an easy win for White) **7.Nxg6+ 8.Nxh4**, and a win for White. Value: 5 points. If you saw that 1.h8=Q is good for Black, give yourself 1 point, but if you didn't find 1.Nf4, you get no further credit.

TEST 132: At first glance, this position looks completely hopeless for White because he can't prevent Black from crowning his h2-pawn with check. However, White has only one pawn that can move, so he plays for stalemate with **1.h7+ Kh8 2.Bg7+ Kxh7** (now White has no more pawn moves, but his King seems to have plenty of places to go to) **3.Ba1+!** (excellent—this move takes the a1-square away from the White King and simultaneously deprives the Bishop of any moves) **3...Kg6 4.Rxc6+ Kh5 5.Kb2!!** (the goal of White's play: when Black promotes his pawn, White's King will have no legal moves) **5...h1=Q** (forced, because White threatens to stop the promotion with Rc1; White now gets rid of his last mobile piece) **6.Rh6+! Kxh6** Stalemate! Value: 5 points. A tough test! What's more, you get credit only for the answer given!

TEST 133: White can force checkmate by placing Black's King in a stale-mated position so that any check is checkmate. This is the solution: **1.Qg5+!! Bxg5 2.hxg5+ Kh5** (Black thinks he is safe because the pinned pawn prevents White from playing g4) **3.Rh8!** (threatening ...Rxh7 Check-mate) **3...Qxh8** (abandoning the pin) **4.g4** Checkmate. Value: 3 points.

TEST 134: The enticing **1...Rxc3??** looks like a winning possibility, but it is actually a losing blunder. Black sees that 2.Qxc3?? Qb1 leads to checkmate and 2.bxc3?? Qxc2 drops the White Queen. So how can such a first move be bad? Look to Black's back rank for the answer: **2.Rd8+ Bf8 3.Bf4!!** (giving the White King a place to run to and also threatening 4.Bh6 with a quick checkmate) **3...Qa5** (after 3...Qa1+ 4.Kh2 Rxc2 5.Bh6, Black will be check-mated) **4.Rxf8+ Kxf8 5.Qxc3**. Down a piece, Black gives up after a few more moves. Value: 3 points.

TEST 135: Black expects the defensive 1.Be2, but instead White shatters the pin by jumping to the attack: **1.Nxe5! Bxd1 2.Bb5+ c6** (after 2...Nd7 3.Bxd7+ Qxd7 4.Nxd7, White ends up with an extra piece) **3.dxc6** (threat-ening discovered checks with 4.c7 or 4.cxb7) **3...Qb6** (also hopeless for Black is 3...a6, which leads to a White win after 4.c7+ axb5 5.cxd8=Q+ Rxd8 6.Nxd1) **4.cxb7+ Qxb5 5.bxa8=Q+**. Black resigns. Value: 3 points.

TEST 136: A celebrated combination. The great Rubinstein starts by sacrificing some pieces to draw White's Queen away from the defense of the e4-Bishop: **1...Rxc3!! 2.gxh4** (2.Bxc3?? leads to 2...Bxe4+, when Black can't recapture on e4 because of ...Qxh2 Checkmate) **2...Rd2!!** (the second shock) **3.Qxd2** (3.Bxc3 loses instantly to 3...Bxe4+ 4.Qxe4 Rxh2 Checkmate; a similar result occurs with 3.Bxb7 Rxe2 4.Bg2 Rh3! 5.Bxh3 Rxh2 Checkmate and with 3.Qxg4 Bxe4+ 4.Rf3 Rxf3 5.Qg2 Rf1+ 6.Rxf1 Bxg2 Checkmate) **3...Bxe4+ 4.Qg2 Rh3!** White resigns because he cannot defend against checkmate on h2. Value: 5 points. If you found 1...Rxc3 and 2...Rd2, give yourself 1 point. If you also worked out the consequences of all the lines other than 3.Qxd2, give yourself 2 points. If you saw the tricks with Rh3, take 4 points.

TEST 137: White starts a magnificent combination based on the poorly defended Black Queen, the vulnerable Black King, and the loosely defended Black Rook on c8. The c8-Rook is attacked by White's c1-Rook and x-rayed by White's Queen. Here's how: **1.Rxe7+!! Kf8!** (countering with a threat of back rank checkmate—now every White piece is hanging; worse was 1...Qxe7 2.Rxc8+ Rxc8 3.Qxc8+, with an easy win; also hopeless was 1...Kxe7 2.Re1+ Kd6 3.Qb4+ Kc7 4.Ne6+ Kb8 5.Qf4+ and a win for White) **2.Rf7+! Kg8** (2...Qxf7 is still impossible because 3.Rxc8+ wins a Rook) **3.Rg7+!** (the indestructible Rook makes a funny impression; if Black captures the Rook with his King, White captures Black's Queen with check) **3...Kh8 4.Rxh7+!**. At this point, Von Bardeleben realized he had lost and stormed out of the tournament hall. He didn't return and forfeited the game. Steinitz then showed the spectators how the game would have ended: **4....Kg8 5.Rg7+ Kh8** (5...Kf8 leads to the winning 6.Nh7+ Kxg7 7.Qxd7+) **6.Qh4+ Kxg7 7.Qh7+ Kf8 8.Qh8+ Ke7 9.Qg7+ Ke8 10.Qg8+ Ke7 11.Qf7+ Kd8 12.Qf8+ Qe8 13.Nf7+ Kd7 14.Qd6** Checkmate. Value: 5 points. Give yourself 1 point for 1.Rxe7, another point for realizing that 3...Kh8 is forced and that 3...Kf8 allows the winning 4.Nxh7+ Ke8 5.Nxf6+. Give yourself a third point for sacrificing a Rook with 6.Qh4+.

Key to Tactical Tests

0–15 points   I'll be honest with you, this is not good. You need to carefully read this book again.

16–21 points   This is a solid, respectable score. You have a good grasp of basic tactics.

22–42 points   Congratulations! You have mastered basic tactics.

43–60 points   You are a master tactician.

61–90 points   Impressive! The average master lives in awe of you.

91–100 points   You can tactically hold your own with some of the best players in the world.

101 and higher   Warn me if we play, and I'll make a point of keeping the game simple and boring.

Glossary

Active: In relation to an opponent's style, denotes a preference for aggressive or tactical types of play. Otherwise, means an aggressive move or position.

Advantage: A net superiority of position, usually based on force, time, space, or pawn structure.

Algebraic notation: Many ways of writing chess moves have been devised over the years. In fact, there are probably as many ways of writing chess moves as there are languages. However, algebraic notation has become the international standard.

Essentially, each square on the chessboard is given a letter and a number. The files are assigned the letters a, b, c, d, e, f, g, and h, from left to right from White's perspective. The ranks are assigned the numbers 1, 2, 3, 4, 5, 6, 7, and 8, from bottom to top from White's perspective. Thus, the bottom left corner is square a1 and the top right corner is square h8.

When a piece travels from one square to another, algebraic notation enables you to identify the piece and the square to which it is moving. For example, if the Rook moves from square a1 to square a8, you write Ra8. For pawn moves, you write only the square to which the pawn moves; for example, e4. Castling Kingside is written O-O, and castling Queenside is written O-O-O. In this book, algebraic notation is sometimes referred to as *chess notation* or simply *notation*.

Analysis: The calculation of a series of moves based on a particular position. In tournament play, you are not allowed to move the pieces during analysis but must make all calculations in your head. When the game is over, opponents commonly analyze the game they have just played, moving the pieces about in an effort to discover what the best moves would have been.

Annotation: Written comments about a position or game. The comments can take the form of narrative, chess notation, or a combination of both.

Attack: To start an aggressive action in a particular area of the board, or to threaten to capture a piece or pawn.

Battery: Doubling Rooks on a file or a Queen and a Bishop on a diagonal creates a battery.

Berserker: A playing style characterized by frenzied attacks with one or two pieces. Named after ancient Scandinavian warriors who worked themselves up into battle frenzies and then charged their opponents with little regard for strategy or personal danger.

Bishop pair: Two Bishops vs. a Bishop and a Knight or two Knights. Two Bishops work well together because they can control diagonals of both colors. *See also* Opposite-colored Bishops.

Blockade: To stop an enemy pawn by placing a piece (ideally a Knight) directly in front of it. Popularized by Aaron Nimzovich.

Blunder: A terrible move that loses material or involves decisive positional or tactical concessions.

Breakthrough: Denotes a penetration of the enemy position.

Calculation of variations: The working out of chains of moves without physically moving the pieces.

Castle: A player castles by moving his King and Rook simultaneously. Castling is the only move in which a player can deploy two pieces in one move. Castling allows a player to move his King out of the center (the main theater of action in the opening) to the flank, where the King can be protected by pawns. Additionally, castling develops a Rook.

When White castles Kingside, he moves his King from e1 to g1 and his h1-Rook to f1. When Black castles Kingside, he moves his King from e8 to g8 and his h8-Rook to f8. When White castles Queenside, he moves his King from e1 to c1 and his a1-Rook to d1. And when Black castles Queenside, he moves his King from e8 to c8 and his a8-Rook to d8.

Center: The center is the area of the board encompassed by the rectangle c3-c6-f6-f3. Squares e4, d4, e5, and d5 are the most important part of the center. The e- and d-files are the *center files*.

Checkmate: An attack against the enemy King from which the King cannot escape. When a player checkmates his opponent's King, he wins the game.

Classical: A style of play that focuses on the creation of a full pawn center. Classical principles tend to be rather dogmatic and inflexible. The philosophy of the classical players was eventually challenged by the so-called "hypermoderns." *See also* Hypermodern.

Clearance sacrifice: A move that sacrifices an obstructing piece to make way for a strong move.

Closed game: A position that is obstructed by blocking chains of pawns. Such a position tends to favor Knights over Bishops, because the pawns block the diagonals.

Combination: A sacrifice combined with a forced series of moves, which exploits specific peculiarities of the positions in the hope of attaining a certain goal.

Connected passed pawns: Two or more passed pawns of the same color on adjacent files. *See also* Passed pawn.

Control: To completely dominate an area of the board. Dominating a file or a square, or simply having the initiative, can constitute control.

Counterplay: When the player who has been on the defensive starts his own aggressive action.

Cramp: The lack of mobility that is usually the result of a disadvantage in space.

Critical position: An important point in the game, where victory or defeat hangs in the balance.

Decoy: A tactic that lures an opponent's piece to a particular square.

Defense: A move or series of moves designed to thwart an enemy attack. Also used in the names of many openings initiated by Black. Examples are the French Defense and the Caro–Kann Defense.

Deflection: A tactic that involves chasing the opponent's main defending piece away from the critical area so that the defense falls apart.

Development: The process of moving pieces from their starting positions to new posts, from which they control a greater number of squares and have greater mobility.

Discovered attack: A discovered attack is an ambush. A Queen, Rook, or Bishop lies in wait so that it can attack when another piece or pawn moves out of its way.

Discovered check: A discovered attack that involves checking the enemy King.

Double attack: An attack against two pieces or pawns at the same time.

Double check: A discovered attack that checks the King with two pieces. The King is forced to move, and the enemy army is thus frozen for at least one move.

Doubled pawns: Two pawns of the same color lined up on a file. This doubling can only come about as the result of a capture.

Draw: A tied game. A draw can result from a stalemate, from a three-time repetition of position, or by agreement between the players. *See also* Stalemate; Three-time repetition of position.

Elo rating: The system by which players are rated. Devised by Professor Arpad Elo (1903–) of Milwaukee and adopted by FIDE in 1970. A beginner might have a 900 rating, the average club player 1600, a state champion 2300, and the World Champion 2800.

En passant: A French term that means *in passing*. When a pawn advances two squares (which it can do only if it has not moved before) and passes an enemy pawn on an adjacent file that has advanced to its 5th rank, it can be captured by the enemy pawn as if it had moved only one square. The capture is optional and must be made at the first opportunity; otherwise, the right to capture that particular pawn under those particular circumstances is lost.

Endgame: The third and final phase of a chess game. An endgame arises when few pieces remain on the board. The clearest signal that the ending is about to begin is when Queens are exchanged.

Equality: A situation in which neither side has an advantage or the players' advantages balance out.

Exchange: The trading of pieces, usually pieces of equal value.

Exchange, The: *Winning the Exchange* means you have won a Rook (5 points) for a Bishop or a Knight (3 points).

FIDE: The acronym for *Fédération Internationale des Échecs*, the international chess federation.

File: A vertical column of eight squares. Designated in algebraic notation as the a-file, b-file, and so on. *See also* Half-open file; Open file.

Flank: The a-, b-, and c-files on the Queenside, and the f-, g-, and h-files on the Kingside.

Force: Material. An advantage in force arises when one player has more material than his opponent or when he outmans his opponent in a certain area of the board.

Forced: A move or series of moves that must be played if disaster is to be avoided.

Fork: A tactical maneuver in which a piece or pawn attacks two enemy pieces or pawns at the same time.

Gambit: The voluntary sacrifice of at least a pawn in the opening, with the idea of gaining a compensating advantage (usually time, which permits development).

General principles: The fundamental rules of chess, devised to enable less advanced players to react logically to different positions. Also used more often than you would think by Grandmasters!

Grande combination: A combination that involves many moves and features many types of tactics.

Grandmaster: A title awarded by FIDE to players who meet an established set of performance standards, including a high Elo rating. It is the highest title (other than World Champion) attainable in chess. Lesser titles include International Master and FIDE Master, which is the lowest title awarded for international play. Once earned, a Grandmaster title cannot be taken away. *See also* Elo rating; Master.

Half-open file: A file that contains none of one player's pawns but one or more of his opponent's.

Hang: To be unprotected and exposed to capture.

Hole: A square that cannot be defended by a pawn. Such a square makes an excellent home for a piece because the piece cannot be chased away by hostile pawns.

Hypermodern: A school of thought that arose in reaction to the classical theories of chess. The hypermoderns insisted that putting a pawn in the center in the opening made it a target. The heroes of this movement were Richard Réti and Aaron Nimzovich, both of whom expounded the idea of controlling the center from the flanks. Like the ideas of the classicists, those of the hypermoderns can be carried to extremes. Nowadays, both views are seen as correct. A distillation of the two philosophies is needed to cope successfully with any particular situation. *See also* Classical.

Initiative: When you are able to make threats to which your opponent must react, you are said to *possess the initiative*.

Interpose: To place a piece or a pawn in between an enemy attacking piece and the attacked piece.

Intuition: Finding the right move or strategy by "feel" rather than by calculation.

Kingside: The half of the board made up of the e, f, g, and h files. Kingside pieces are the King, the Bishop next to it, the Knight next to the Bishop, and the Rook next to the Knight. *See also* Queenside.

Luft: A German term that means *air*. In chess, it means *to give the King breathing room*. It describes a pawn move made in front of the King of the same color to avoid back rank mate possibilities.

Major pieces: Queens and Rooks. Also called *heavy pieces*.

Master: In the US, a player with a rating of 2200 or more. If a player's rating drops below 2200, the title is rescinded. *See also* Grandmaster.

Mate: Short for *checkmate*.

Material: All the pieces and pawns. A *material advantage* is when a player has more pieces on the board than his opponent or has pieces of greater value. *See also* Point count.

Middlegame: The phase between the opening and the endgame.

Minor pieces: The Bishops and Knights.

Mobility: Freedom of movement for the pieces.

Occupation: A Rook or Queen that controls a file or rank is said to *occupy* that file or rank. A piece is said to occupy the square it is sitting on.

Open: Short for *open game* or *open file*. Also refers to a type of tournament in which any strength of player can participate. Though a player often ends up with opponents who are stronger or weaker than himself, the prizes are usually structured around different rating groups, with prizes for the top scorers in each group. Such open tournaments are extremely popular in the United States. *See also* Open file; Open game.

Open file: A vertical column of eight squares that is free of pawns. Rooks reach their maximum potential when placed on open files or open ranks.

Open game: A position characterized by many open ranks, files, or diagonals and few center pawns. A lead in development becomes very important in positions of this type.

Opening: The start of a game, incorporating the first dozen or so moves. The basic goals of an opening are to
- Develop pieces as quickly as possible.
- Control as much of the center as possible.
- Castle early and get the King to safety, while at the same time bringing the Rooks toward the center and placing them on potentially open files.

Openings: Established sequences of moves that lead to the goals outlined under Opening. These sequences of moves are often named after the player who invented them or after the place where they were first played. Some openings, such as the *King's Gambit* and the *English*, have been analyzed to great lengths in chess literature.

Opposite-colored Bishops: Also *Bishops of opposite color*. When players have one Bishop each and the Bishops are on different-colored squares. Opposite-colored Bishops can never come into direct contact.

Overextension: When space is gained too fast. By rushing his pawns forward and trying to control a lot of territory, a player can leave weaknesses in his camp, or can weaken the advanced pawns themselves. He is then said to have *overextended* his position.

Overworked piece: A piece that is required to single-handedly defend too many other pieces.

Passed pawn: A pawn whose advance to the 8th rank cannot be prevented by any enemy pawn and whose promotion to a piece is therefore inevitable. *See also* Promotion; Underpromotion.

Pawn structure: Also referred to as the *pawn skeleton*. All aspects of the pawn setup.

Perpetual check: When one player places his opponent in check, forcing a reply, followed by another check and another forced reply, followed by another check that repeats the first position. Because such a game could be played forever, after the position repeats itself, the game is declared a draw. *See also* Three-time repetition of position.

Perpetual pursuit: Similar to a perpetual check, except that the pursued piece is a Bishop, Knight, Rook, or Queen, instead of the King.

Petite combination: A combination that involves only a few moves.

Pig: Slang for *Rook. Pigs on the 7th* is a common term for Rooks doubled on the 7th rank.

Pin: When one player attacks a piece that his opponent cannot move without losing a different piece of greater value. When the piece of greater value is the King, this tactic is called an *absolute pin*; when it is not the King, the tactic is called a *relative pin.*

Plan: A short- or long-range goal on which a player bases his moves.

Point count: A system that gives the pieces the following numeric values: King—priceless; Queen—9 points; Rook—5 points; Bishop—3 points; Knight—3 points; and pawn—1 point.

Positional: A move or style of play that is based on long-range considerations. The slow buildup of small advantages is said to be positional.

Prepared variation: In professional chess, it is common practice to analyze book openings in the hope of finding a new move or plan. When a player makes such a discovery, he will often save this prepared variation for use against a special opponent.

Promotion: Also called *queening*. When a pawn reaches the 8th rank, it can be promoted to a Bishop, Knight, Rook, or (most commonly) Queen of the same color. *See also* Underpromotion.

Protected passed pawn: A passed pawn that is under the protection of another pawn. *See also* Passed pawn.

Queenside: The half of the board that includes the d-, c-, b-, and a-files. The Queenside pieces are the Queen, the Bishop next to it, the Knight next to the Bishop, and the Rook next to the Knight. *See also* Kingside.

Quiet move: An unassuming move that is not a capture, a check, or a direct threat. A quiet move often occurs at the end of a maneuver or combination that drives the point home.

Rank: A horizontal row of eight squares. Designated in algebraic notation as the 1 (1st) rank, the 2 (2nd) rank, and so on.

Rating: A number that measures a player's relative strength. The higher the number, the stronger the player. *See also* Elo rating.

Resign: When a player realizes that he is going to lose and graciously gives up the game without waiting for a checkmate. When resigning, a player can simply say, "I resign," or he can tip over his King in a gesture of helplessness. When you first start playing chess, I recommend that you never resign. Always play until the end.

Romantic: The Romantic (or Macho) era of chess from the early to mid-1800s, when sacrifice and attack were considered the only manly ways to play. If a sacrifice was offered, it was considered a disgraceful show of cowardice to refuse the capture. Today, a player who has a proclivity for bold attacks and sacrifices, often throwing caution to the wind, is called a *romantic.*

Royal fork: A fork that attacks the King and Queen.

Sacrifice: The voluntary offer of material for compensation in space, time, pawn structure, or even force. (A sacrifice can lead to a force advantage in a particular part of the board.) Unlike a combination, a sacrifice is not always a calculable commodity and often entails an element of uncertainty.

Simplify: To trade pieces to quiet down the position, to eliminate the opponent's attacking potential, or to clarify the situation.

Skewer: A threat against a valuable piece that forces that piece to move, allowing the capture of a piece behind it.

Smothered checkmate: When a King is completely surrounded by its own pieces (or is at the edge of the board) and receives an unanswerable check from the enemy, he is said to be a victim of Smothered checkmate.

Space: The territory controlled by each player.

Space count: A numerical system used to determine who controls more space, in which 1 point is allocated to each square on one player's side of the board that is controlled by a piece or pawn belonging to the other player.

Speculative: Made without calculating the consequences to the extent normally required. Sometimes full calculation is not possible, so a player must rely on intuition, from which a speculative plan might arise.

Stalemate: In the English language, a stalemate refers to a standoff between opposing forces. In chess terminology, a stalemate occurs when one player is so bottled up that any legal move he makes will expose his King to immediate capture. A stalemate results in a draw (a tied game).

Strategy: The reasoning behind a move, plan, or idea.

Study: Theoretical positions, or *compositions*, that highlight unusual tactical themes.

Style: Players approach chess in different ways as a result of their personalities and preferences. The types of move a player chooses are usually indicative of the player as a person. Typically, in a game between players of opposing styles (for example, an attacker vs. a quiet positional player), the winner will be the one who successfully imposes his style on the other.

Tactics: Maneuvers that take advantage of short-term opportunities. A position with many traps and combinations is considered to be *tactical* in nature.

Tempo: One move, as a unit of time; the plural is *tempi*. If a piece can reach a useful square in one move but takes two moves to get there, it has *lost a tempo*. For example, after 1.e4 e5 2.d4 exd4 3.Qxd4 Nc6, Black gains a tempo and White loses one because the White Queen is attacked and White must move his Queen a second time to get it to safety.

Theory: Well-known opening, middlegame, and endgame positions that are documented in books.

Three-time repetition of position: Occurs when the players have been moving back and forth, repeating the same position. Often happens when a player, behind in material and facing eventual loss, sacrifices for a perpetual check (*see* Perpetual check). A three-time repetition of position results in a draw (a tied game).

Time: In this book, in addition to the common use of the word ("Black does not have time to stop all of White's threats"), time is a measure of development. Also refers to *thinking time*, as measured on a chess clock. *See also* Time control; Tempo.

Time control: The amount of time in which each player must play a specified number of moves. In international competitions, the typical time control is 40 moves in 2 hours for each player. After each player has made 40 moves, each is given an additional amount of time (usually 1 hour for 20 moves). If a player uses up his time, but has not yet made the mandatory number of moves, he loses the game by forfeit, no matter what the position on the board.

Time pressure: One of the most exciting moments in a tournament chess game. When one or both players have used up most of their time but still have several moves to make before they reach the mandatory total of 40 or 45, they start to make moves with increasing rapidity, sometimes slamming down the pieces in frenzied panic. Terrible blunders are typical in this phase. Some players get into time pressure in almost every game and are known as *time-pressure addicts*.

Transposition: Reaching an identical opening position by a different order of moves. For example, the French Defense is usually reached by 1.e4 e6 2.d4 d5, but 1.d4 e6 2.e4 d5 *transposes* into the same position.

Trap: A way of surreptitiously luring the opponent into making a mistake.

Underpromotion: Promotion of a pawn to any piece other than a Queen.

Variation: One line of analysis in any phase of the game. It could be a line of play other than the ones used in the game. The term *variation* is frequently applied to one line of an opening; for example, the Wilkes–Barre Variation (named after the city in Pennsylvania) of the Two Knights' Defense. Variations can become as well-analyzed as their parent openings. Entire books have been written on some well-known variations.

Weakness: Any pawn or square that is readily attackable and therefore hard to defend.

Zugzwang: A German term that means *compulsion to move*. It refers to a situation in which a player would prefer to do nothing because any move leads to a deterioration of his position, but he moves something because it is illegal to pass.

Zwischenzug: A German term that means *in-between move*. A surprising move that, when inserted in an apparently logical sequence (for example, a check that interrupts a series of exchanges), changes the result of that sequence.

Index

A

absolute pins, 35–38, 41, 60, 87, 89, 100, 209–10
active, 235
advanced combinations, 201, 203
advantage, 235
Alekhine, Alexander, 30, 45, 152, 157, 163–73, 175, 185
Alekhine's Defense, 30
algebraic notation, x, 235
analysis, 235
Anderssen, Adolf, 135–43, 145–46, 151, 156, 167
Andersson, Ulf, 189
annotation, 236
attacks, 236
  discovered, 9, 15, 84, 141, 153, 199, 207, 223, 238
  with pawns, 32
  against squares, 205
  and x-rays, 111, 113
  double, 6, 9, 22–32, 69, 108, 113, 147, 205, 238
  and batteries, 82
  by pawns, 29–32
  mating, 242
Averbakh, Yuri, 6

B

back rank
  checkmates, 66–69, 112, 136, 150–62, 215, 223, 241
  and batteries, 82
  Kings on, 66

back rank, *continued*
  weak, 68–69, 76, 220, 224
  and x-rays, 111
basic tactics, 199
batteries, 79–88, 161
Berry, Jonathan, 107
Bishops
  on adjacent diagonals, 87
  forks, 20
  hanging, 11
  on open diagonals, 85–86
  opposite-colored, 243
  pairs, 236
  and Queens on diagonals, 86
  and Rook-Pawn vs. King, 128–29
blockades, 124–25, 236
blunders, 236
Botvinnik, Mikhail, 5, 106, 175, 185
Bradford, Texas Joe, 29
breakthrough, 236
  combinations, 91–93
building fortresses, 119, 122–30, 221
Burns, Amos, 158

C

Capablanca, José Raúl, 40, 157, 163, 166, 209
captures, forced, 105–6, 208
capturing en passant, 239
castling, 61, 154, 165, 193
  Kingside, 237
  purpose of, 236
  Queenside, 237

castling, *continued*
  rule, 236
  center, 237
Chajes, O., 164
chaturanga, 85
checks
  discovered, 12–14, 59, 114, 205, 214, 238
  double, 15, 55, 142, 206, 214, 224, 238
  perpetual, 57–60, 118, 150, 243, 247
  vs. pursuit, 119
  premature, 26
  when to avoid, 26
checkmate, 237
  back rank, 66–69, 112, 136, 150, 162, 178, 215, 223
  and batteries, 82
  discovered, 215
  double, 15
  pure, 140
  smothered, 54–55, 245
chess conventions, 3–7
chess notation. *See* algebraic notation
chess terms, 3–7
classical, 237
clearance sacrifices, 105–9, 156, 162, 217
closed
  files, 79
  games (*see* positions, closed)
combinations, 4–5, 14, 237
  advanced, 201, 203
  breakthrough, 91–93

combinations, break-
through, *continued*
sacrifices in, 92
involving Kings, 51–69
petite, 23, 33
recognizing, 6–7
connected passed pawns.
See pawns, connected
passed
conventions, 3–7
correspondence chess, 18
counterplay, 238
cramp, 238
critical positions. *See* positions, critical

D
decoys, 99–103
defenses, 238. *See also* openings (*or individual de-
fense names*)
deflection, 73–78, 181, 216
destroying King's cover,
61–65, 161
development, 145–147
definition, 238
diagonals
Bishop and Queen on, 86
Bishops on adjacent, 87
doubling on open, 79
open, 79, 85–87, 146
discovered
attacks, 9, 15, 141, 153,
199, 207, 223, 238
with pawns, 32
against squares, 205
and x-rays, 111, 113
checkmate, 15, 215
checks, 12–15, 55, 59, 114,
142, 205, 206, 214,
224, 238
double attacks, 6, 9–33, 69,
108, 113, 147, 205, 238
and batteries, 82

double attacks, *continued*
by pawns, 29–32
doubled Rooks on 7th, 80,
228, 244
doubling
on open files, 101
on open lines, 79
Rooks, 211
draws, 89, 119–30. *See also*
stalemates; three-time
repetition of position
definition, 239
forcing, 124
material imbalance, 126–29
perpetual check, 57–60
stalemate, 51–55
three-time repetition, 58,
119, 169

E
Elo rating, xi, 239
Elo, Arpad, 239
en passant
example of, 83
rule, 239
endgame, 239
English Opening, 164, 186
equality, 239
Evans Gambit, 140
Evergreen Game, The, 140
Exchange, the, 12, 42, 85,
166, 170, 205–6,
208–9, 224, 239
exchanging, 239

F
Fédération Internationale
des Échecs (FIDE),
xi, 239
FIDE, xi, 239
files, 239
closed, 79
doubling on open, 79, 101

files, *continued*
half-open, 79, 83, 240
open, 79–83, 242
Fine, Reuben, 29, 151,
157, 170
Fischer, Bobby, 26, 163,
169, 185
Flamberg, Alexander
Davidovich, 152
flank, 239
Forbis, 179
force, 3, 240. *See also* material
forced, 240
captures, 105–6, 208
moves, 146
forcing
draws, 124
moves, 113, 121, 162
to specific squares, 99
stalemates, 128
trades, 152
forks, 9, 18–26, 69, 75, 80,
101–2, 168, 170–71,
199, 206–8, 223
Bishop, 20
as combinations, 22
King, 21
Knight, 4, 19, 23–24
pawn, 31–32, 53, 208
Queen, 21
Rook, 20
royal, 19, 23, 96, 101–2,
107, 187, 218
underpromoting to create,
95
fortresses, building, 119,
122, 221
French Defense, 154, 238,
247

G
gambits, 151, 158, 171, 240
Gheorghiu, Florian, 192

Grandmaster (GM), 240
Gurgenidze, Bukhuty
    Ivanovich, 182

H
half-open files, 79, 83, 240
hanging, 240
  Bishops, 11
  Knights, 37, 74
  Queens, 225
heavy pieces, 241
hole, 241
Hort, Vlastimil, 66
Hübner, Robert, 186
hypermodern, 167, 241

I
Immortal Game, The, 136
initiative, 237, 241
international chess federa-
    tion, xi, 239
International Master (IM),
    240
interposition, 21
intuition, 241

K
Karpov, Anatoly, 185, 192
Kasparov, Garry, 163,
    185–95
King's Gambit, 137
Kings
  and absolute pins, 35
  on back rank, 66
  vs. Bishop and Rook-Pawn,
    128–29
  and castling, 61
  destroying cover of, 61–65,
    161, 213
  drawing into hostile terri-
    tory, 61–64
  forks, 21

Kings, *continued*
  keeping out, 122
  vs. Knight and Rook-Pawn,
    127–28
  making luft for, 67
  open, 51
  relative strength of, 122
  stalemated, 7
  tactics and combinations
    involving, 51–71
  vs. two Knights, 126–127
  weak, 6, 51
Kingside, 241
Knights
  forks, 4, 19, 23–24
  hanging, 37, 74
  and Rook-Pawn vs. King,
    127–28
  two, vs. King, 126–27

L
Lasker, Emanuel, 4, 11, 97,
    114, 157, 163, 171, 206
L'Hermet, R., 154
luft
  definition, 241
  making, 67

M
major pieces, 241
Marshall, Frank, 157–62
Master, 241
mate, 242. *See also* check-
    mate
material
  advantage, 240, 242
  definition, 240
  imbalances, 126–29
  point count system, 244
middlegame, 242
Miller, J., 176
minor pieces, 242
mobility, 242

Modern Benoni System, 182
Morphy, Paul, 143, 145–50,
    156, 167
moves, 243–46
  forced, 146, 162
  forcing, 113, 121
  passive, 243

N
Nimzovich, Aaron, 45, 89,
    236
notation. *See* algebraic
    notation

O
occupying squares, 242
open
  diagonals, 79, 85–87, 146
    doubling on, 79
  files, 79–83
    doubling on, 79, 101
    pins on, 211
  games. *See* positions, open
  Kings, 51
  positions. *See* positions,
    open
openings, 242–43
  and absolute pins, 35
  Alekhine's Defense, 30
  and Alexander Alekhine,
    163
  Caro–Kann Defense, 238
  English Opening, 164,
    186, 243
  Evans Gambit, 140
  French Defense, 154, 238,
    247
  gambits, 137, 140, 151,
    158, 171, 240
  and Garry Kasparov, 185
  King's Gambit, 137, 243
  Modern Benoni System,
    182

openings, *continued*
  names of, 30
  Philidor Defense, 146
  Queen's Gambit Declined,
    158, 171
  Queen's Indian Defense,
    Petrosyan System,
    189, 193
  Scandinavian Defense, 36
  Sicilian Opening
    Dragon Variation, 180
  Tarrasch Defense, 160
  Two Knights' Defense,
    176, 248
  Vienna Opening, 152
opposite-colored Bishops.
    See Bishops, opposite-
    colored
overextending, 243
overworked pieces, 73, 215

P
Parsons, Jeffrey, 55
passed pawns. *See* pawns,
    passed
pawn
  chains, 237
  structure, 3
    static factor, 246
pawns
  backward, 236
  capturing en passant, 239
  connected passed, 237
  as defenders, 74
  discovered attacks with, 32
  double attacks by, 29–32
  doubled, 238
  forks, 31–32, 53, 208
  passed, 91, 120, 218, 243
    connected, 91
    protected, 244
  passing through, 91
  poisoned, 244
  power of, 89–97

pawns, *continued*
  promoting, 89–96, 218,
    224, 231, 243–44 (*see
    also* pawns, un-
    derpromoting)
  protected passed, 244
  queening potential of, 31
  sacrificing, 120, 137, 141
  for Rooks on 7th, 80
  and stalemate, 127
  stopping, 236
  strength from weakness,
    29–30
  trading for pieces, 31
  underpromoting, 94–96
    (*see also* pawns, pro-
    moting)
    to avoid stalemate,
      94–95
    to create forks, 95
    reasons for, 94
perpetual
  checks, 57–60, 118, 150
    (*see also* checks, per-
    petual)
  vs. pursuits, 119
  pursuits, 119–121, 221
    vs. checks, 119
    definition, 243
petite combinations, 23
Petrosyan System of
    Queen's Indian De-
    fense, 189, 193
Petrosyan, Tigran, 185
Philidor Defense, 146
Philidor, François-André
    Danican, 41, 146
philosophies
  classical, 237
  hypermodern, 241
pieces
  as defenders, 74–75
  heavy, 241
  major, 241
  minor, 242

pieces, *continued*
  overworked, 73, 215
  trapping, 129–30
  undefended, 7, 74
pigs, 244
  on 7th, 80, 244
pins, 15, 35–45, 69, 100, 142,
    148, 165, 199, 206,
    208, 210, 215
  absolute, 35–38, 41, 60, 87,
    89, 100, 209–10
  and batteries, 82
  on open files, 211
  relative, 35, 38, 41–43, 209
  vs. skewers, 47
Pipe Game, The, 158
plans, 244
playing styles, 246
point count system. *See*
    material, point count
    system
  in tournaments, 51
positional
  concepts, 151
  definition, 244
  players, 175
positions
  closed, 237
  cramping, 238
  critical, 238
  open, 242
  passive, 243
  sharp, 245
  simplifying, 245
  wild, 248
powerful pawns, 89–96
prepared variations. *See*
    variations, prepared
preventing sacrifices, 158
principles, 240
promoting pawns, 89–96,
    218, 224, 231. *See also*
    pawns, promoting
promotion, 244. *See also*
    pawns, promoting

protected passed pawns. *See* pawns, protected passed
pure checkmate, 140
pursuits, perpetual, 119–21, 221
vs. check, 119
definition, 243

Q

Queen's Gambit Declined, 158, 171
Queen's Indian Defense, Petrosyan System, 189, 193
queening, 31, 89–93, 218. *See also* pawns, promoting
Queens
and Bishops on diagonals, 86
creating from pawns, 89–93
developing too early, 36
forks, 21
hanging, 225
sacrificing, 11, 24, 62, 64, 68, 76, 86
vulnerability of, 121
Queenside, 244

R

ranks, 245
rating, 245. *See also* Elo rating
recognizing tactics and combinations, 6–7
relative pins, 35, 38, 41–43, 209
Reschevsky, Sammy, 119
resigning, 245
Reti, Richard, 167
romantic, 245

Rooks
doubled on 7th rank, 80, 228
doubling, 211
ensuring activity of, 80
forks, 20
as King hunters, 63
on 7th rank, 79, 216
doubled, 80, 228
sacrificing pawns for, 80
royal forks, 19, 23, 96, 101–2, 107, 187, 218, 245
Rubinstein, Akiba Kiwelowicz, 160, 233

S

sacrifices, 5, 9, 14, 22, 159, 208
in breakthrough combinations, 92
clearance, 105–9, 156, 162, 217, 237
and decoys, 99–102
definition, 245
to draw out Kings, 61–62
pawn, 120, 137, 141
for Rooks on 7th, 80
preventing, 158
for promotion, 89, 91
Queen, 11, 24, 62, 64, 68, 76, 86
for stalemate, 52–53
Scandinavian Defense, 36
7th rank
double Rooks on, 80
importance of, 81
pigs on, 80
Rooks on, 79
sacrificing pawns for, 80
Sicilian Opening
Dragon Variation, 180

Silman, Jeremy, 6
Silman's Rules of Recognition, 6, 10, 14, 207
simplification, 212. *See also* trading
simultaneous games, 176, 179
skewers, 47–49, 166, 199, 208, 211
definition, 245
vs. pins, 47
smothered checkmate, 54–55, 245
Smyslov, Vasily, 56, 175
space, 3
advantage, 236
count system, 246
definition, 246
static factor, 246
Spassky, Boris, 94, 185
Spielmann, Rudolf, 151–56, 157
squares, occupying, 242
stalemates, 7, 51–55, 85–86, 149, 212–13
and a- and h-pawns, 127
motion, 94–95
definition, 246
forcing, 128
perils of, 64
sacrifices to achieve, 52–53
undesirable, 54
Steinitz, Wilhelm, 140, 143, 233
strategy, 246
structure, pawn, 3
studies, 17
style. *See* playing styles

T

tactics, 3–4
basic, 199
definition, 246

tactics, *continued*
  double attacks, 9–32
  forks, 18
  involving Kings, 51–69
  recognizing, 6–7
Tal, Mikhail, 107, 175–84,
  185
Tarrasch Defense, 160
tempo, 246. *See also* time
terms, 3–7
theory, 247
three-time repetition of position, 58, 119, 169, 213,
  247
tied game. *See* draws
time, 246
  controls, 247
  definition, 247
  limits, 247
  loss of, 246
  pressure, 247
tournaments, point count,
  xi, 51
trades, forcing, 152
trading, 74, 138
  advantages of, 13
  even, 36
  exchange, 239
  pawns for pieces, 31
  simplification, 212
transposition, 247
trapping pieces, 129–30
traps, 168, 247

Troitzky, Alexei Alexeyevich,
  17
Two Knights' Defense, 176,
  248

U
undefended pieces, 7, 74
underpromoting, 218
  definition, 248
  pawns, 94–96
    to avoid stalemate, 94–95
    to create forks, 95
    reasons for, 94

V
variations
  calculating, 236
  definition, 248
  prepared, 244
Vienna Opening, 152
Von Bardeleben, Curt, 233

W
weak
  back rank, 68–69, 76,
    220, 224
    and x-rays, 111
  King, 6, 51
weaknesses, 248
windmills, 111, 114–15, 220

Wizard of Riga, 107
World Champions
  Alekhine, Alexander, 30, 163
  Botvinnik, Mikhail, 5, 106,
    175, 185
  Capablanca, José Raúl,
    166, 209
  Fischer, Bobby, 26, 185
  Karpov, Anatoly, 185, 192
  Kasparov, Garry, 185–95
  Lasker, Emanuel, 4, 11, 114
  rating of, 239
  Smyslov, Vasily, 175
  Steinitz, Wilhelm, 140
  Tal, Mikhail, 107, 175–84

X
x-rays, 111–13, 220, 233
  and discovered attacks,
    111, 113
  and weak back rank, 111

Y
Youngworth, Perry, 103

Z
zugzwang, 210, 248
zwischenzug, 117–18, 121,
  225, 248

Yasser Seirawan

International Grandmaster Yasser Seirawan is considered the top US contender for the chess World Champion title. The only American contender for the world title since Bobby Fischer retired in 1975, Seirawan has earned numerous titles, including 1979 World Junior Champion, three-time US Champion, 1989 Western Hemisphere Champion, and five-time member of the US Olympic chess teams. In tournament play, he has defeated both Garry Kasparov and Anatoly Karpov, the two top-ranking players in the world. He is the only American to have played in the World Cup cycle.

Born in Damascus, Syria, in 1960, Seirawan moved to Seattle at the age of seven. His chess career was launched at the age of twelve, when he began to play in (and win) local and regional tournaments. Seirawan lives in Seattle, Washington, where he is the editor of *Inside Chess* magazine. Readers are invited to write to: Inside Chess, P.O. Box 19457, Seattle, WA 98102, for a complimentary copy.

Jeremy Silman

International Master Jeremy Silman tied for first place in the 1990 National Open tournament. He also tied for first place in the 1982 US Open. He is a former Pacific Northwest Champion and a former Washington State Champion.

Silman has written extensively about chess. He is the author of 16 books, and his magazine articles have been published all over the world. He has produced a video and a computer program. Silman now lives in Beverly Hills, California.

The manuscript for this book was prepared and submitted to Microsoft Press in electronic form. Text files were processed and formatted using Microsoft Word.

Principal word processor: Christina B. Smith
Principal proofreader: Polly Fox Urban
Principal typographers: Zaafar Hasnain/Uli Schumm
Interior text designers: Darcie S. Furlan/Kim Eggleston
Principal illustrator: Jeanne Reinelt
Cover designer: Rebecca Johnson
Cover illustrator: Henk Dawson
Cover color separator: Color Control

Text composition by Online Press Inc. in Century Old Style with display type in Optima Bold, using Ventura Publisher and the Linotronic 300 laser imagesetter.

Printed on recycled paper stock.